"Kudos for introducing another needed component of teacher preparation. This book is a wonderful way for a new teacher to have insight on possible scenarios that most educators experience. It is a surprisingly easy read yet a potent lesson on the professionalism lessons that are not taught in education courses. This book also adds the perfect story format with real world application for monitoring with a new teacher mentor teacher pair. Awesome job!"

—Kim Richardson, Instructional Supervisor, Hampton City Public Schools, Hampton, VA

"I feel that reading Sara's journey has confirmed a secret about quality communication or conversation that if I really want to know about someone or something, ask questions. Then listen, really listen because the answers may not be what I already know. So the motive of my heart has to be to know the person, not just the task or information. Quality conversation leads to relationship."

—Donna Hines, Home school teacher/ Ministry Leader, Chesapeake, VA

"This book reflected how I was during my younger years and now as an adult I see how the four pillars were what I needed to be successful in my life and in the marketplace. Also, it is helpful as I raise my two young men."

—Carol Boone, a Deputy Treasurer, Suffolk, VA

As a principal, I often look for strategies to use to improve upon my professional practices. At the heart of success rests positive relationships. To build effective relationships, you must be able to have all types of conversations with those around you. By utilizing the strategies in this work, I constantly engage in conversations of quality that are honest, focused, supportive, but most importantly reflective.

—Tracey Flemings, Principal,
Lafayette-Winona Middle School, Norfolk, VA

EMPOWERING WORDS

Apostle Eric Miller

Continue to speak
empowering words to the
people of God and inspire
them to live for Him.
God's blessings be upon
you and your family!

A.J.

3/26/12

GALE A. LEE and ALICE M. SPENCE

EMPOWERING WORDS

Transforming
the Way We Talk

A Parable

TATE PUBLISHING
AND ENTERPRISES, LLC

Published by Tate Publishing & Enterprises, LLC
127 E. Trade Center Terrace | Mustang, Oklahoma 73064 USA
1.888.361.9473 | www.tatepublishing.com

Tate Publishing is committed to excellence in the publishing industry. The company reflects the philosophy established by the founders, based on Psalm 68:11,
"The Lord gave the word and great was the company of those who published it."

Book design copyright © 2012 by Tate Publishing, LLC. All rights reserved.
Cover design by April Marciszewski
Interior design by Nathan Harmony

Published in the United States of America

ISBN: 978-1-61862-308-9
1. Education / Leadership
2. Education / Professional Development
11.12.19

Dedication

To our colleagues in education around the globe and to the teachers who touched our lives—especially our parents, Jessie Lee, Jr. and Eddye J. Lee and Alice Coles Johnson and the late Caliph Coles.

Acknowledgements

"Recognition of the existence or truth of something." I recognize that there are many who had it not been for their existence in my life, the possibility exists that my conversational experiences may have gone unchanged. I am grateful for their existence and their impartation of truth. It is their engagement of me and their conversations with me about what I saw as truth that transformed me.

To my parents, Jessie Lee Jr. and Eddye J. Lee: I love you. At an early age you helped me recognize the brilliance of and damaging effects of my tongue. Thank you. You have taught me to be quieter than I had to be and kinder than I wanted to be through your modeling. These are important tenets that you exhibit and share with me daily. Employing these tenets enabled me to learn how to control my tongue and develop the self-control I needed to develop myself professionally. Thank you for the insights and truths that you share with me as you observe me. It is always helpful. I look forward to them forever.

To my brother Bill (aka William, Tony): you always see the best in me. Even when I am a not to happy camper, you ask me questions that help me think deeper than I planned to think. Your questions and insights often linger in my memory. Thank you for being that voice that has helped me develop the practice of reflecting deeply.

To my brother Don: It's good that we both have a sense of humor because sometimes life's medicine is bitter. Thanks for laughing with me and listening.

To Amber: Watching you grow and develop been amazing. Watching you engage others in conversations has been even more amazing. Thank you for your support of my work. I encourage you to continue the good work and remember you are my number one!

To Alice my co-author: What a wonderful journey! We have experienced every opportunity to apply the tenets of quality conversation. From listening, to asking powerful questions, and giving and receiving LOTS of constructive feedback, we can continue to reflect on this wonderful work and enjoy the rewards of impacting the world. Thanks, my friend. You are the best.

Dr. Joseph Umidi, thanks for helping me answer the "how". How do I engage others fully? How do I get results through my conversations? How do I move beyond what has been self-taught to refining and building my conversational style using the gift of teaching? You are a great teacher who recognizes and understands that within each of us is the answer. Also, thank you for developing the *LifeForming* curriculum. It has changed my life and the lives of those who commit to engaging the principals of having a quality conversation through the use of coaching techniques. I promise you that I will commit to touching thousands of lives through the use of these strategies and hope that, through my modeling, millions will feel your passion for coaching and engaging in quality conversation.

To Darlene Mack and Successful Innovations, Inc; thank you for your continued support and encouragement. Your passion is inspiring and motivational. I look forward to greater collaboration.

From Alice: When I think of all the people who inspired, influenced, encouraged, and empowered me to write this book, the list could go on and on. So, I thank everyone and especially the following people:

I thank God for creating the gift of encouragement and communication in me and for allowing me to write this book. I thank Gale, my co-author and friend! Wow, we did it! Thank you for having genuine and authentic quality conversations with me about every subject for nearly twenty years. I thank my mother, Alice Mae Johnson, who has always been there for me through her love, patience, guidance, understanding, and encouragement, and for allowing me to engage adults as a youngster even when "children were to be seen and not to be heard." I thank my family, especially my siblings Henry, Caliph, Mattie, Lillie, Inell, Odell, and David for letting me know from the very beginning that I could communicate and sometimes a little too much! To Mrs. Mary Conyers, my 8th grade English teacher, thank you for building my confidence in writing, public speaking, and always encouraging me to fulfill my life purpose. To my spiritual parents and teachers, George Jones, C. B. and Jackie Haskins, Rosetta Lee, and Lonell Maddux, thank you for speaking encouragement and empowerment into my life when

I needed it the most throughout my adolescence and young adulthood.

To my daughter, Joselyn, you are the greatest and thanks for being there for me regardless of the situation or circumstance and for bringing the imagination of our cover into reality for us. To Nyia, my 85 pounds grand pit bull puppy, thanks for energizing me with all those licks, especially during those times when I wanted to stop writing. You kept me writing on!

I thank our mentor Dr. Joseph Umidi for challenging Gale and I to further refine the art of quality conversations with leaders in the marketplace and places of worship through *Lifeforming* leadership coaching and to write the book from our experiences!

I thank Bishop B. Courtney McBath, Pastor Harold and Lady Brenda McPherson, and my church family at Covenant Community Church in Suffolk, Virginia, for the prayers, words of encouragement, and support. Also, I thank Sharon Schiff, my former intern, and Amber Lee, for reading the first few pages and Brother Alonzo Robinson for taking those young ladies' voices and creating a CD so that others could listen to our work and give further input.

I thank my friends and book reviewers: Fredia Rene Alexander, Carol Boone, Donna Hines, Gloria Lassister, Sheryl Gonzales, Marilyn Yochum, Pat Tabron, Annette Sivels, Paula Conyers-Walker, Betty Washington, Trish Parker, Kathy Butler, Sharion Wilson, Deborah Ingram, Angela Myers, and Angelia Washington for your prayers, insight, and encouragement throughout this project.

I thank all of my former and current principals, Dr. Cathy Lassister, Mrs. Jeanne Krueger, and Mrs. Tracey Flemings, for encouragement and allowing me the opportunity to present to staff and others at conferences and meetings about the positive results of having quality conversations.

I thank the people at Tate Publishing for your encouragement and excitement about this project, especially Donna Chumley, our acquisition editor. Your suggestions have made the difference. I thank Sylvia Davis, for her expertise in editing and reviewing our manuscript.

I thank all of my spiritual children, students, parents, and colleagues at all of the schools I have served for allowing me to engage you every single day in having quality conversations and for giving me insightful and valuable feedback.

Our work has been about building personal and professional relationships while achieving positive results by having quality conversations. We have tested this work in our personal lives and the results are amazing. It is our belief that this book will do the same for you!

Foreword

"The conversation is the relationship!" I never could figure out what that meant with my wife and children until I learned the value of courageous, committed, collaborative conversations. I thought that the quality of relationships at home and at work could be evaluated by other more important behaviors than the quality of the conversations in those relationships. At least that is what I needed to believe to keep myself in the silent mode for so many of those long car drives and too many of those meal times.

It is getting better all the time today. That is because of the stories we have gathered from twenty countries and twelve languages where the principles of this book were first put to the test. What we discovered in every culture, age group, gender, socio-economic status, ethnicity, and nation was that conversations could be the key to connection. That connection can be a more powerful bridge than any of the forces that seek to divide families, communities, vocations, and yes, even nations.

In one of my trips to South Africa, we had to change our training program for professional coaches when foreigners from other African nations were driven out of home and businesses with little help in that first critical week from the

15

host government. It was then that I saw the power of what we came to call *Real Talk Training* in an environment when small talk, shop talk, idle talk, and spin talk could not hold back the rage of poverty and abandonment seeking to vent itself on something that could relieve the pressure of persevering pain. That week I taught hundreds of community workers the principles of connecting that became an effective method to establish, protect, and produce meaningful relationship, even with foreigners who they had grown to only tolerate instead of celebrate in their neighborhoods. Today there is an army of conversational coaches in South Africa who are providing real talk, creative talk, and breakthough talk that is recreating a culture of honor in the ashes of a culture of shame.

I am honored to see where this book will now take you, the reader. It is the legacy of the hundreds of coaches we have trained to go into the key vocations that can advance the quality of those cultures by excelling the quality of our conversations. This book launches these powerful concepts in the realm of education where a conversation makes the difference between becoming a civic leader or a gang member, just-get-by mentality and a just-give-me-a-chance mentality.

The first fruit of this transformational paradigm will be seen in the quality of the conversations amongst teachers and staff, most notably in those places where they gather together away from their students. This is the report I received from training school principals and teachers with these principles back in 2007.

The next wave of results will be like a tsunami of refreshing waters over the conversations between teachers and parents. There is no doubt that this book and its principles will not only minimize destructive conflict but will maximize the benefits of a conflict process that is mediated by one's effective use of powerful questions and listening to what really matters.

But the greatest return on investment will be the subtle shift in the schoolyard where students who have tasted the real thing with real talk will move away from the bully and belittling talk that has been the norm far too long. I confidently predict that defensiveness will be disarmed, and a new sense of collaboration will emerge amongst the student bodies in our schools who see their leader teachers make the shift that enable them to follow in their own peer relationships.

Sounds like a potential over promise and under deliver…except for one thing. My life has been changed by these principles and practices. The professionals we have trained with these are now going far beyond what we dreamed in multiplying the effects of these in the hard places of our culture.

I commend the authors of this book. They live what they teach and they have given you a slice of their life in this well-written manuscript. Read and beware; you will be ruined for the ordinary and will not settle for anything daily but the extra-ordinary in the teacher's lounge, classroom, boardroom, homeroom, and even at the dinner table. This real talk is for real…just ask my wife and kids!

—Dr. Joseph Umidi
Founder/President
Lifeforming Leadership Coaching

Introduction

Quality conversations have always posed a challenge for me, especially in the workplace. However, if I am to judge by the plethora of stories that I am privy to, it is safe to say that I am not alone. My parents' voices still resonate from my childhood, telling me, "Gale, watch your tongue." That phrase remains to this day a reminder to think before I speak. Over the course of my career it has compelled me to develop and focus on some of the conversational pillars that I now hold near and dear to my heart.

My struggle with conversations began early. As a child I could be described as an introvert. It was not easy for me to engage people in conversation. I was categorized as not being a people person but I would later discover that this was inaccurate. My problem was that I did not understand how to engage others in meaningful conversations. My awkward attempts usually made me look like a pubescent conversationalist, never saying the right thing.

As an adult, my obsession with conversations climbed to a whole new level of importance. When I began my first real job as an educator I learned that I would need to acquire the skills necessary to have conversations with a whole new group of peers—and it wasn't going to be easy. As a brand new professional just out of college, with my "know-everything" and "can-teach-anybody" attitude, I was about to experience a steep learning curve unlike anything I had known before. Remember that pubescent conversationalist I mentioned earlier? Well here it was again—not a great personality attribute to have as an educated twenty-something adult.

I loved my class and teaching, and held my administrators in great esteem, but I dreaded the conversations with my peers. It was not a great surprise that my evaluation indicated that I needed to improve my engagement with the other teachers. The test began. How could I eliminate this obstacle and move towards fulfillment or at least learn how to participate in a conversation that would build up instead of break down? What to do? I knew things could be a lot better. I needed to change. I realized that the way I engaged in conversations could make me or break me. My ability to communicate would directly impact my destiny.

Then I met my co-author, Alice. She is quite the opposite of me, as it relates to conversations. Alice is the pure definition of an extrovert! I'm sure you Myer-Briggs folks understand what I am saying. We connected through a ministry effort, in a meeting with our pastor to discuss the writing of a grant. I expressed to our pastor the need to get results. This is, after all, what an INTJ is after. Alice, on the other hand, was very quiet at this particular meeting. It was a surprise to find out later what a conversational extrovert she really was!

We had work to do, and she had some very valuable contributions. It was through a conversation with Alice

20

that I decided to take the risk and ask her to hold me accountable for the phrase my parents instilled in me, "Gale, watch your tongue." Having a safe person to help me identify my conversation patterns has helped me mold and shape my conversational self from within. The outward expression of this process has been very productive and rewarding for me and I believe that I have also contributed to others.

Remember, everyone's conversation is valuable.

—Gale

Okay, Gale has described me as a true extrovert. Well, here's the reason. I grew up on a tobacco and vegetable farm in rural Virginia and was privileged to be the last of ten children (five girls and five boys). I came from a lineage of storytellers and farmers. You would think that the youngest would be quiet and shy. Oh, no! In fact, I was the most outgoing, friendly, and talkative of all the children. I loved having conversations. You could find me on any given day walking or running through the tobacco fields and orchards, or feeding the chickens and pigs, asking anyone who would listen questions about everything and anything. I thrived on understanding and new knowledge. My mother often told me that I was a different kind of child. Once she said to me that I would never be lost in this world because I knew how to find my way through communication. But not every comment was that supportive. Possibly without meaning any harm, family members would make comments, such as, "Girl, don't you get tired of talking?"

or "You overwhelm people sometimes with all of those questions," and even "You wear me out talking!" I was very young, still developing and discovering myself, and these comments cut like a knife.

Mostly, however, the balance has been positive. I can say that I have never met a stranger because I am never a stranger to others. I easily befriend people and sometimes even made some friends that my family did not approve of because I am hardwired to enjoy talking, listening, and helping others. People gravitate to me because I listen and am able to make them feel better about their situation, no matter what it is. Gale has truly been a great friend and coach to me. I am able to clearly express my thoughts and feelings openly and authentically. Her feedback has brought balance, clarity, and a better focus to my conversations, thereby enriching the overall quality of my life and for that I am deeply grateful.

—Alice

We know that effective conversations impact lives in the most intimate and defining ways. They influence our self-esteem, our relationships, and can improve our metacognition. Do you want to feel better emotionally and physically? Improve your conversations. Do you want to make your employees feel relevant? Improve your conversations. Do you want to increase productivity and have more useful evaluation conferences? Improve your conversations. Measure yourself (because others will) by the quality of your conversations. As you engage those around you in focused conversations, you will:

- Produce life and build up people
- Engage people to become creative and positive
- Motivate and empower others
- Increase self-esteem and confidence
- Develop leaders and great employees

Think carefully when you communicate. Pay close attention to your communication patterns and take the risk to find someone safe to hold you accountable for your conversations. This feedback will help you refine and develop a deep appreciation for the art of quality conversations. As educators we are aware of the statistics related to the high attrition of teachers with three to five years of experience and it breaks our hearts. But we also know that one way we can possibly turn the tide of teacher attrition is to have quality conversations and build relationships.

If you are ready to adjust and refine your conversational patterns, come along with us on this conversational journey through the eyes of Sarah, a brand new teacher who learns (just in time) the value of engaging in quality conversations.

—Gale and Alice

Part I: Sarah's Story

The landing announcement shook Sarah from her day-dream. She looked out the aircraft window at the Dallas skyline against the crisp blue winter sky. As Sarah reached down to tuck her handbag under the seat in front of her, turbulence jolted the whole fuselage and pressed the buckle of her seatbelt into her stomach. Sarah felt her heart pump faster. She looked over to the passenger next to her but the teenager didn't even look up; he seemed just as relaxed as before, sorting through the song list on his iPod. *The sky was so clear, there was not a cloud out there*, Sarah thought, *and yet there can always be an unforeseen risk, something unknown*. The plane landed smoothly and soon Sarah was in her rental car, driving for the next four hours to her hometown of Winnsboro. While she did not enjoy flying, driving relaxed her. The open road and the radio had a meditative effect. She was spending Thanksgiving with her parents and it was her first visit home since her new teaching job had started. Her younger sister Gayle and her new husband Noah would be there too.

"So how's the new job?" Her father handed her a cup of coffee across the kitchen table.

"Not too bad," Sarah replied.

"That's it?" her father insisted, "after ten weeks of teaching kids it's just …not too bad? Are the kids out of control? What's the matter with kids these days?"

"The kids are fine…" Sarah started to reply but her mother interrupted playfully, slapping her husband with a kitchen towel.

"Let Sarah breathe, honey," she said, "She's been driving for hours. Give her a break." Her father sighed. Sarah had always had a close connection with him; words almost weren't necessary. She couldn't hide anything from him; she knew he would sense it. He could probably tell something wasn't right with her job, but the moment passed, and she let the matter remain unspoken. She had not had time to deal with it herself. So many years of education and preparation building up to her first proper teaching job and here she was, a few months into it and already falling flat on her face. Gayle swung open the kitchen door carrying a huge platter of food.

"Sarah!" Her sister set down her cargo and swept Sarah up in a warm hug.

"Where's your husband?" Sarah asked.

"My husband! I love to hear you say that," she said, "He's just gone to get some ice. He'll be here in a minute."

It was still odd to think of her little sister as a wife, but it hadn't been a surprise when the engagement was announced. Gayle was only nineteen when she walked down the aisle, but she had always had a clear dream of what the future held for her. She wanted a pretty house near her parents and a husband who would work on her father's farm, of course, and four children, two boys and

26

two girls. So far she had gotten the house and the farmer husband, and Sarah suspected that it wouldn't be long before a baby was on the way. Sarah felt a sense of safety knowing that Gayle had such a firm grip on life. It gave her wings to venture out and take a job far away from home, knowing that her parents would always have Gayle and the farm would always have Noah.

"So what's up?" Gayle poured herself a cup of coffee.

For the first time Sarah felt like a guest in her parents' house. Seeing how Gayle moved comfortably in the kitchen, knowing what needed to be done, made the feeling more pronounced. Gayle was tightly knit into the fabric of their everyday life. Sarah, on the other hand, had chosen the road less traveled. She was the first one in her family to obtain a college degree, the first one to move away to a big town, the first one to become a teacher.

"You didn't miss much," her father said, shrugging his shoulders. "I was asking Sarah about her job but apparently I shouldn't trouble her."

"Mom made you shut up," Gayle said, laughing, "Come on, Sarah, how's the job going? Tell us about the big city. What's your apartment like? Have you met any cute guys yet?"

The kitchen door opened again quietly and Sarah welcomed the sight of Noah. He hesitated at the door for a second, scanning the room with his big brown eyes. Noah had a bullfighter's natural grace about him, and he was chronically unrushed.

"It's so good to see you, Sarah!" Noah said, hugging her lightly, "Happy Thanksgiving!"

"Happy Thanksgiving, Noah,"

27

"How's the new job?"

"Oh, well…"

"She doesn't like it," her father interjected.

"I'm sorry to hear that."

"She didn't say that she didn't like it," her mother chimed in, "did she now?"

"Do you, Sarah?" Gayle pressed, "Do you like it?"

"Of course she doesn't like it," her father said, "I know my girl."

"How come?" her mother said, , " I don't understand."

"Now you're making Mom worry," Gayle said , "What's wrong with the job anyway?"

Sarah took a deep breath and gathered the empty coffee cups and took them to the sink.

"Nothing." Sarah looked to Noah for support.

"Hey Gayle," Noah said, "guess who's car I just saw in the Parker's driveway?"

"No way!"

"Yep, it must be getting serious if he's spending Thanksgiving with her folks."

With that smooth diversion the conversation swerved away from Sarah and into the matchmaking rituals of people who are not married and therefore must be helped. Sarah smiled at her sister, a creature alight with the sheer joy of living. Sarah knew, however, that she would not be able to hold off the subject of her teaching job for much longer. She was not quite ready to say what unfortunately would have to be said, because if she announced it out loud it would make it real. She knew her news would spoil Thanksgiving. *Not yet. Not yet.*

28

First Impressions

The first few days of the new job had been nerve-wracking for Sarah but exhilarating at the same time. She was still riding on the cloud of receiving the signed contract for her job in one of the few Blue Ribbon Schools of Distinction, no meager achievement for a teacher fresh out of college. Sarah was used to being at the top of her game. In college she had made the Dean's List each semester. She had aced every single interview and gotten an offer from the one school she really wanted to work for, Jackson Elementary School, the top rated school in the greater Houston area. She had become a minor celebrity in her hometown when her mother announced proudly to everyone in the phone book of their small town that her daughter was going to teach at such an important institution. Besides the school's amazing reputation and standing, Sarah had taken an instant liking at Mr. Coles, the principal. He was a veteran educator but was also relatively new to Jackson as this was only his second year in this school. From the first telephone interview Mr. Coles and Sarah had clicked, and she was smart enough to know that Mr. Coles was going out on a limb to select her over the other five candidates with longer résumés. He was putting a great deal of faith in her academic performance and her potential. Sarah was determined not to disappoint him, but as the saying goes, "If you want to make God laugh, make a plan." The first hurdles came right at the pre-service week at school. Minutes after Sarah picked up her keys at the main office she was already busy decorating her 4th-grade classroom with colorful borders and organizing her bulletin boards. As Sarah was crawling under her desk to retrieve tape she'd dropped, the door opened and a portly lady came in, teetering on high heels with her platinum hair impeccably swept up in a bun.

"Hello, I'm Margie Taylor."

"Hi," Sarah said, reversing on all fours from under the desk, "I'm Sarah Granger."

"I know, I am your grade level chair."

"It's nice to meet you. I've just started getting organized."

"Yes, well, I stopped by to say hello before the meeting."

Sarah gave her a blank look.

"We have a meeting in ten minutes."

"Oh, I wasn't aware."

"Maybe you didn't get a copy of the agenda when you got your keys?" Margie said, "I'll have an extra copy for you at the meeting."

"Sure."

As soon as Margie left, Sarah spotted the meeting agenda on the desk. She had arrived with her arms full of stuff and had just plopped everything on the desk and hadn't noticed there was a letter there. *You only have one chance to make a first impression*, she thought. Sure enough, the meeting was clearly marked as the first order of the day. Sarah locked up and made her way to the appointed room. Walking down the halls, she felt positive about her choice of school. Such a magnificent place! She found the room and saw the rest of the staff was already there.

"...on this new initiative..." Margie stopped mid-sentence. "Come in Sarah. Everyone, I want you to meet Sarah Granger, the newest member of our team. Please show her the ropes and look out for her. Right. Where was I? Yes, as I was saying, this is just one of the new initiatives and we need to move forward..."

Margie continued going over point after point listing initiatives and requirements, such as differentiated instruction, tier instructions, character education, and family engagement. Sarah zoned out after a while because it so much to take in. There was an information package handed over in an orange binder for each team member and after a perfunctory request from Margie for everyone to go over the information carefully in their own time, the meeting adjourned. Sitting on the edge of her chair, Sarah quickly flipped through the thick stack of papers and silently scanned the endless list of requirements and changes. Everyone came up to greet Sarah and then one by one they left, until there was only one teacher left. He came up and extended his hand.

"I'm Ed," he said. "I'm new too."

"Great, I'm not the only newbie!" Sarah said, shaking his hand.

Sarah looked up at his green eyes; she guessed he must be in his early to mid-thirties, tall and thin.

"I don't mean I'm new at teaching. I'm just new to the school. I moved here from Seattle."

31

"I've never been to Seattle. "I've always wanted to visit."

"I suppose it is a nice enough place," Ed said with a clipped smile, "good coffee, and lots of rain."

Sarah nodded but couldn't help staring at the wedding ring on his finger. She felt herself blushing. *Had he caught her look? What would he think?*

"Well," Ed said, "I better get moving. If there's anything I can help you with, anything at all, just let me know."

Sarah made a mental note to steer clear of Ed in the future. No complications at work. For the rest of the day and late into the evening Sarah devoted herself to reading the orange folder with the information package.

The following morning she woke up with a headache. She had read every page twice and was now more confused than ever. With a turkey sandwich and an apple, Sarah set off for work feeling more overwhelmed than the day before. She busied herself organizing the classroom and took some more time to read over the instructions again. They still didn't make sense. Around noon she ventured into the teacher's lounge for the first time. There were a handful of people there. The teacher who had just finished using the photocopier walked towards Sarah with papers flapping around.

"You must be the new fourth grade teacher," she said, smiling. "I'm Amy."

She sat down next to Sarah and opened her lunch bag. As they both bit into their sandwiches, Amy chatted away easily. She was a veteran sixth grade teacher and had formerly been a 4th grade teacher like Sarah, so they already had something in common.

"I've been doing all the talking," she said, "How are you liking Jackson so far?"

"It's wonderful!" It's such a beautiful school, and it has such a good reputation."

"It does, "and it deserves it."

"I don't have much to say yet. This is my first job."

"Fantastic!" Amy said, "You couldn't be in better hands. Principal Coles is very experienced, and the whole team is very supportive. I am positive you'll love it. Please let me know if I can do anything to help, anything at all. Never hesitate to come and talk. As you can probably tell, I don't mind talking!"

Sarah laughed and thought of telling Amy about her struggle with the information package .

"Actually," Sarah said and hesitated.

"Yes?" she asked.

"Nothing. Everything's fine; it's just a lot to take in."

"Of course. It's just the beginning. Ease into it; don't let yourself get overwhelmed. Remember I'm always here if you need anything."

"Thanks, Amy, I really appreciate it."

Sarah returned to her classroom. The brief conversation with Amy should have made her feel better but somehow she felt uneasy. She knew that she was on par with everyone else here academically. Sarah couldn't quite put her finger on what was weighing on her. Maybe it was that everybody else seemed to be so at ease with their jobs, even Ed who technically was also new to Jackson. The real work hadn't even started yet. Next week classes would begin, the students would arrive, and the parents would rightly expect her to hit the ground running. She

33

was not even able to follow the instructions from her team leader. How would Margie evaluate Sarah's performance? How would she know what the expectations were? Sarah decided to go to Margie for clarification. It was not a good idea to start on such shaky footing. Just as she thought this, Margie appeared in the corridor rushing in the opposite direction on clicking stilettos.

"Hey Sarah," she said.

"Margie, could I have a word?"

"Oh, sure," Margie said, "I was just heading out. How can I help you?"

"In the orange folder you gave us," Sarah said, "which requirement would you say would be the initial focus for the first month of school?"

"Did you read it?" Margie asked.

"Yes."

"Already?" Margie said, shifting her feet and shooting a glance towards the door.

"Yes, all of it," Sarah said, "three times."

"Three times!" Margie said, "You'll know it by heart soon! Just prioritize as you were trained, then I'll let you know if anything needs to be corrected."

Margie trotted off at an alarming speed for her pointy shoes. Sarah was left standing in a daze. Was she expected to fumble in the dark until she made a mistake and only then she would be corrected? Was this Margie's idea of leadership? Trial and error? Sarah felt her shoulders tense up. Her thoughts rushed . It was only when she turned to leave that she saw Ed coming out of his classroom. Had he overheard?

34

Transitions

When the children arrived, Sarah felt her anxiety melt into the background. She fell back on her student teacher-training experience, where she had consistently performed at the top of her class and had earned stellar recommendations from her mentors and advisor. While her confidence grew in the classroom, the cloud of concern regarding her team leader continued to loom darker over her enjoyment of the job. That Friday, as Sarah was leaving for the day, she came across Principal Coles in the parking lot.

"So how's it going, Sarah?"

"Pretty good," Sarah said, walking with him, "The children are lovely. I have such a diverse group."

"That's one of the things that makes Jackson so special, that and our staff. You have such a great grade-level chair; Margie has such experience and balance."

Sarah kept silent. They had reached Mr. Coles's car.

"She'll be a great resource for you."

"Well," Sarah said, "I'm not sure that I can follow everything Margie is setting out just yet."

"Ah, I expect it will get better. From my first interview with you, Sarah, I knew your potential. You can handle a challenge. There's a bright future ahead for you."

35

"Thank you, I'm enjoying it here, and I don't want to give you the wrong impression."

"Give yourself some time to settle," Mr. Coles said, getting into his car, "it can be a bit overwhelming at the beginning."

As he was driving away, he paused and turned to Sarah.

"Oh, Sarah," he said, "if you don't want to give me the wrong impression, give me the right one."

With a blink and a wave he was off, leaving Sarah to figure out the meaning of his words. In the following days, Sarah kept bumping into Mr. Coles in hallways, the cafeteria, and in between scheduled meetings. He always had an encouraging word for her.

Before long Sarah had firmly banished Margie's complicated orange folder to the bottom drawer of her filing cabinet. Out of sight; out of mind. It had become clear to her that there was no love lost between her and Margie. Sarah enjoyed teaching and, in her eyes, that was her job. If she was not meeting Margie's indecipherable priorities, then Margie would have to approach her. *If Margie expected to be chased and begged for clear directions then she had another thing coming,* she thought. Sarah was becoming increasingly anxious every time she attended the weekly team meetings because she felt that she was not on the same level as everyone else. She could hardly avoid attending, but in order to cope she sat as far away from Margie as possible and pretended to make notes to avoid eye contact. The strategy seemed to be working, at least for the time being, but it was making Sarah tense and withdrawn . The feeling continued to build up until the

36

day before Thanksgiving break, when Margie asked Sarah to stay behind after class. Margie entered the empty classroom and waited for Sarah to finish tidying up.

"How can I help you?" Sarah said, brushing a wisp of hair from her face.

"I noticed that you are not participating in our meetings." I'm concerned about your lack of communication."

"*My* lack of communication?" Sarah asked, her eyes widening.

"I also haven't received any feedback from you regarding the priorities and initiatives for the first semester, and I am running behind in my reporting."

"Margie, I don't know what to say.

"I'm just asking you to think about it," Margie said, "we can talk when you get back. Are you visiting your family?"

"Yes, I'm flying to Dallas and then driving home. It's a long drive."

"It'll be nice to go home. Happy Thanksgiving, Sarah, and keep up the good work."

Keep up the good work! What was that supposed to mean? Was she being sarcastic? Sarah felt her cheeks getting hotter. *Why wasn't anybody else complaining about Margie? Was she the only one to see the lack of direction in her team?* It was all meaningless now. Enough. She knew what to do. On the way out of the school building Sarah came across Mr. Coles. He was carrying a filing box with both hands and his briefcase dangling from the middle finger of his left hand.

"Let me help you with that," Sarah said.

"Thanks! I just need to get this to the car".

"Taking work home?"

"I'm afraid so," Mr. Coles said, and laughed, "There's a thought for people who think that teaching happens in the classroom!"

"Yes, the classroom is the easy part."

"Oh? Are you having any difficulties with the rest?"

Sarah didn't reply. They got to the car and Mr. Coles plopped the box in the back seat and took the briefcase back from Sarah.

"Thanks," he said, "now I can wish you Happy Thanksgiving properly. Enjoy your holiday."

"Thank you, Mr. Coles. Don't mind what I said. I didn't mean anything in particular."

'*But…*"

"No buts."

"There's always a *but*. I hope you know that you can talk to me whenever you have any questions or anything is not right."

"I know. I've thought about it…"

"But…" he said.

They both laughed.

"You're right," she said, "there's a but."

"Go on," Mr. Coles said, leaning against the car.

Sarah thought for a moment about telling Mr. Coles about the decision she had reached but she decided this was not the right time.

"You know what," she said, "it's not that urgent. Could we maybe have a meeting after the holidays?"

"Of course."

"I appreciate that."

38

"Let me share something with you. Do you have a minute?"

"Of course," Sarah said.

Mr. Coles dove into the backseat of his car and rummaged through some papers. He emerged holding up a few pages stapled together. He pointed to a bench under a laden apple tree, a sight that reminded her of home.

"Here," he said, "lets sit for a moment. When I took over last year there had been an interim principal here and things weren't exactly peachy. I tried a tool that has given me great results."

Mr. Coles explained how the communication lines among the different teams had been neglected for years. The formal tasks were performed without fault but any new idea or anything that fell outside of the strict guidelines were lost in translation. Sarah took the report and leafed through it. She was even more confused. This had nothing to do with the administration procedures, priorities, or initiatives she was struggling with. It was a report simply called "Quality Conversations" and it outlined elements and examples.

"I have used this in my previous school," Mr. Coles said. "It was passed on to me by my mentor. Maybe you can read it over the holidays and we'll talk about it in our meeting when you get back? "

Sarah nodded.

Just Talking

As Gayle and her mother labored in the kitchen, Sarah was recruited to set the table. She enjoyed having something to do and put special care in arranging her mother's beautiful china, silverware, and crystal. She placed a small flower arrangement in the center and candles on each end.

"Wow!" her father said, bringing in the bread and the cranberry sauce. "The table looks great."

They all sat down to eat. Her mother was a very good cook and Gayle had taken after her. The turkey, the stuffing, the yams, everything was made with care and was absolutely delicious. Her father had started a fire in the log burner, although it wasn't really that cold. As the pumpkin pie came out, everyone was getting very full and mellow. The conversation had revolved around the neighbors, the farm and now, inevitably, it had come back to Sarah.

"So when are you coming back home again, Sarah?" her mother asked.

"I don't know."

"You'll be home for Christmas, right?" Gayle said.

"Maybe sooner," Sarah said in a muffled tone, as if announcing the death of a close friend.

41

"Why that's just four weeks away," her father said. "I'm sure you'll be plenty busy, with the Christmas preparations and all?"

A silence descended on the group as Sarah took her time to reply. She gathered her strength and just let it out.

"I'm quitting my job," she said.

The crackling fire was the only sound in the room. Her mother was the first to move, reaching for the dessert platter.

"Pie anyone?" she said.

No one answered, so she served a slice for herself. Gayle looked at Sarah across the table and pursed her lips.

"There's a newsflash," Gayle finally said.

"Sorry to spring it on you like this," Sarah said, "I've been thinking about it for weeks; I just didn't know how to tell you guys."

"Why?" her father said.

"Well," Sarah said, "it's complicated. I love the children. They are really wonderful, and the school is first class and the principal is ..."

"I don't mean that," her father said, pushing his plate away from him. "I mean why didn't you know how to tell us?"

"I just didn't want to upset you," Sarah said.

Sarah noticed that her mother was eating her pie mechanically, in small bites, lost in thought.

"And what are you going to do?" Gayle asked.

"I was planning to come home for now," Sarah said, "maybe help in the farm if you need a hand?"

Her mother stopped her fork in midair. She rested it back on her plate and looked at Sarah with a wounded look.

42

"All that college education and you want to work on the farm?"

"I've heard it all now," her father said. "First farmers are too dumb to understand you and now suddenly we are your new choice of career."

"She never said you were dumb," Gayle said, attempting to rescue Sarah.

"No," her father said, "of course not. She didn't say it, but she implied it."

"And you waited for Thanksgiving to tell us?" her mother asked.

"I just couldn't keep pretending everything was fine."

"Well," her father said, "all the effort to put you through college."

"I'll pay you back," Sarah said.

"With what?" her father said, "It's not about money, you know. You can't put a price on some things."

The volume escalated until her mother left the table, followed by Gayle trying to console her, and her father stormed off to the fields. Sarah went to the kitchen and only Noah remained sitting at the table, alone. As she started to clean up the kitchen and load the dishwasher, Noah came in carrying some dishes.

"That went well," Sarah said, with a half-smile.

"It happens."

They both kept busy, Noah clearing the table and Sarah tidying the kitchen. After a while, Sarah spoke again.

""I don't know what came over me. I wanted to wait for the right time."

43

"It's a lot to keep bottled up," Noah said, "great expectations. You are the golden child."

"No, that's Gayle."

"Gayle is the child they get to keep. You are the child that allows them to dream that anything is possible."

Sarah was struck by the wisdom of Noah's word. He was usually so quiet and reserved.

"So you're quitting," Noah said.

"I'm quitting."

"Have you given notice?" he asked.

"Not yet," Sarah said, "I was planning to do it as soon as I get back."

"Would you like to talk about it?" Noah said.

"Well," Sarah said, surprising herself, "it's rather boring…you don't mind?"

"Coffee?"

"I'd love some."

They sat at the kitchen table as all of Sarah's concerns, feelings, and anecdotes poured out. She told Noah about Mr. Coles, about Margie, even about Ed and Amy, the school, the children, the parents. She described each meeting, every conversation as if she had prepared for a dissertation and she had memorized the presentation word by word. Noah simply nodded along and asked short questions whenever he didn't understand a term or a reference.

"So what you're saying," Noah said, "if I understood correctly, is that although you love the reality of teaching as much as you thought you would, you have been blindsided by the backstage aspects of the job."

44

"Exactly," Sarah said, laughing, "Noah, are you psychic or something?"

"Hardly!" he said, "I was just listening to you."

"You know, I think I'm going to have some of that pie after all,"

She served two thick slices and finished telling Noah about the final conversation with Mr. Coles.

"Can I ask you something more personal Sarah?"

"Go ahead."

"It seems to me from what you said that both Ed and Amy both offered to help you with anything you needed."

"I think I know where you're going with that." Sarah nodded. "Yes, they both did."

"But you never went for them with your questions about your communication problems with Margie."

Sarah thought for a moment. Noah was right.

"In fact," Noah continued, "you haven't even really given the whole picture of the problem to Mr. Coles."

"I didn't want to go behind Margie's back," Sarah said, "I seem to be the only one who has a problem with her, so it would be my word against hers."

"Then it is possible that you haven't given these folks the right impression," he said, "You can't blame them for not getting the message."

Sarah remembered what Mr. Coles had said to her from the car that day.

"That's curious," Sarah said, "the principal one day said to me that if I didn't want to give the wrong impression then I should make sure to give the right one. Maybe that's what he meant."

"Something to think about."

"I guess I better go talk to Mom," Sarah said, "Gayle must be needing a relief pitcher by now."

"Yeah," Noah said, "I'll go and find your Dad."

She got up and then turned back as Noah was preparing to go out.

"Noah," she said, "thank you so much; it felt really good to talk about it."

"Anytime," he said, stepping outside.

Noah being such a good listener, Sarah thought, surely was a solid foundation for a marriage. She went upstairs to find that the mood had already lightened, and Gayle and her mother were sitting on the carpet going through their childhood photos, a favorite family pastime. Sarah's favorite was a picture of her and Gayle sitting up in their apple tree. Gayle looked like pure sunshine with her glistening mahogany curls and her dimpled smile, and Sarah had a reflective look about her, an air of protective big sister. It was a lovely photo.

Later that evening after Gayle and Noah had left and her parents were watching TV, Sarah curled up in an armchair by the fire and read the report that Mr. Coles had given her. It started with some examples of good and bad conversations, how secrets and half-statements can lead to misunderstanding. It described the four pillars of quality conversations:

- Listening
- Asking Questions
- Giving and Receiving Feedback
- Reflection

This was exactly what Noah had done earlier that afternoon. Sarah was struck at how he instinctively knew this. He had listened, he had asked questions when anything was not clear to him, he had then given Sarah a bouncing board for her thoughts, and finally he had summed up his impression very honestly and candidly. Sarah thought back to the argument at the dinner table, how the messages seemed to get crossed and tangled up. In fact Sarah knew from the bottom of her heart that her family had nothing but her best interest at heart. She finished reading the report. She looked over to her parents, sitting side by side on the sofa, with the placid ease that only lifetime companions share. Sarah walked over and nudged her way on the sofa to fit in between them.

"I love you guys," Sarah said.

"We know," her father said and placed his arm around Sarah's shoulder.

"I'm sorry I got so upset," her mother said, folding Sarah's hand in to her own. "You should feel free to make your own decisions."

"I'll give it another try," Sarah said, "The school—I think I haven't given it a fair chance yet."

"Whatever you decide," her father said, "we are with you. We are always just one phone call away."

They kept watching the show, tight in each other's loving warmth, until Sarah spoke softly again.

"You know what," she said, "Gayle knows how to pick a husband. Noah is a first-class guy."

"He's not half-bad," her father said. Sarah knew this to be high praise indeed.

47

EMPOWERING WORDS

Replenishment

The moment Sarah arrived back at her school she headed straight for the teacher's lounge where she knew that she was likely to find Amy. Ed was there too. Sarah called them over to one side.

"I have to ask you a big favor," she said.

They both nodded.

"I need to improve my communication with Margie," Sarah said, "and I don't know how to go about it."

"Is there anything in particular that you are having trouble with?" Ed asked.

"It's everything. It started with the orange folder that detailed all the initiatives and priorities. I have read it several times and still can't really follow, and from then on at every weekly meeting there is something I just don't follow."

"No problem," Ed said, "I can go through the information with you if you'd take me to brunch on a Saturday morning."

Then Sarah asked jokingly, "Can you do that?"

"That reminds me of something," said Amy. "There's a report that Mr. Coles once gave me. It's really good."

"Quality Conversations?" Sarah asked.

"Yes!"

"He gave me a copy to read over the holiday, and I would like to apply that to my meetings with Margie."

"Let's get together at lunch tomorrow, just the three of us," Ed said, "and we could go over both the information package and the report."

"Lunch is on me!"

Feeling like St. George, a knight slaying the dragon, Sarah walked tall to her classroom to set up. At lunch the following day the three got together and discussed Sarah's difficulties. Close to the time to go back to work, Sarah had marked on the margins just three areas where she still had unclear understanding of the initiatives.

"The main thing is," said Amy, "I mean with Mr. Coles the big thing is participation. So many of the initiatives that you are seeing towards the end of the list are long term objectives; they are work in progress. They actually change from one meeting to the next because they are being refined with the feedback from all of us."

"So that's what Margie meant."

"When?" Amy asked.

"Just before Thanksgiving. She said she was lacking my input on things."

"It must be driving her crazy," said Ed.

"That's amazing," Sarah said, looking back over the papers, "I thought that she was driving me up the wall and all this time it has been me who has been a burden on her. It's clear now but just this morning this document was enveloped in a thick fog, and now I've narrowed it down to just three things."

50

"We can write down the questions," said Amy, "so in the next weekly team meeting you are ready to ask Margie exactly what you need."

Ed and Amy helped Sarah turn the three marked areas into three questions and she carefully made notes on her planner.

"Let me guess," Ed said, "You were one of those kids who did so well in college that you never needed to ask for help."

"I'm so glad that you told us about this, Sarah," Amy said, "it really made me feel good to share with you."

"Thank you both," Sarah said, "I think I'm ready for the next meeting with Margie. I can't believe I never asked you about this before. So, you guys didn't have any problems understanding this?"

"Oh, sure," Ed said, laughing, "I was completely clueless. I thought it was just me; you looked so calm and in control."

"So what did you do to understand it?" Sarah said.

"I went to Margie and threw my arms up in the air," Ed said. "She walked me through the entire thing after class one day and pointed out the top three priorities: identification of the needy students, implementing tier instructions, and creating instructional centers in the classroom and told me leave the other ones for later. Like Amy said, closing the achievement gaps and strategies for meeting accreditation standards are evolving so they are bound to change."

"Margie explained it to you?" Sarah said.

"Yes," Ed said, "I think you'll be surprised by her. She probably has no idea that you are struggling with this. You may have given the impression that you have everything under control."

"That is a possibility," Sarah said, "I tend to do that."

Sarah had her doubts that she would ever develop to such a collegial bond with Margie, but she was feeling increasingly confident about her ability to tame the monster of insecurity that had been haunting her for weeks. Ed had a point. In college she had always been at the top of her group, and it was always the others who came to her for support. Now that it was her turn to seek help, she just didn't have the tools to do it.

Sarah came in early at the next weekly meeting. Margie was there, rearranging the chairs to add one more place.

"Mr. Coles may come by today," Margie said. "He likes to sit in on our meetings every now and then."

"Good," Sarah said. "Margie, can I ask you a question?"

Margie finished arranging the chairs, sat down, and waved for Sarah to sit next to her.

"This is a little awkward for me," Sarah said, "I've been thinking over the holidays and I wanted to ask you to…I would like to ask you for your help."

"Of course," Margie said, flashing a wide smile, "what do you need help with?"

"You haven't noticed?"

"Noticed what?" "That half the time I can't follow your meetings," Sarah said, "I've even struggled with the most basic information."

"Well, I noticed that you were not giving me feedback," Margie said, "but I just considered it to be my fault, not yours."

52

"Your fault?"

"It's my job to promote participation," Margie said, "that's why I mentioned it to you last time we talked. I was following up, just doing my job."

"I thought you were pointing out a shortcoming."

"Not at all," Margie said, "in fact you are doing so well that I have no concerns at all about your performance. You took to the classroom like a duck to water. You are set to become one of our great teachers."

Sarah felt her eyes fill up with tears.

"Did I say something to upset you?" Margie said.

Sarah shook her head and brushed off a tear from her cheek. "They're tears of relief. I've built this up in my head. It's been like a black cloud hanging over me, and now it's completely gone. You have no idea how close I came to…well, it's not important now."

"So what did you want to ask me?"

"Well, since I seem to be suffering from overachiever syndrome, I'm finding it difficult to ask you for help when I'm falling behind. So I wondered if you maybe could keep an eye on me, you know, pay a little bit of special attention to me until I get back on a level with the rest."

"Of course I can do that!" Margie said, "and forgive me for not noticing earlier. You seemed to be doing so well. I'm always available after the meeting if you want to stay on for a few minutes whenever you need clarification."

"That's great, Margie, I'll do that. Maybe I'll stay on today after the meeting.

Just then the rest of the group arrived.

"I'm really glad we had this chat," Margie said.

53

"So am I!"

About halfway through the meeting Mr. Coles slipped in quietly and took a seat with them. He did not participate and Margie continued with the discussion as if he wasn't there. After a while he got up and left with just a quick wave to everyone. When the meeting was over, Sarah stayed behind and asked Margie the three questions that she had prepared with Ed and Amy's help. They went through them together and in a matter of fifteen minutes Sarah understood the main areas where she had been confused before. Sarah helped Margie rearrange the chairs and left the room feeling like a weight had been lifted from her shoulders. On her way out, she saw Ed at his desk so she stopped at the doorway and leaned in.

"Hey Ed," Sarah said, "just wanted to thank you again."

"Did it work out with Margie?" Ed said.

"Absolutely," Sarah said, "she was great."

"I figured something was up when I saw you sitting next to her at the meeting," he said, grinning.

"That obvious?" Sarah said, laughing.

"I bet Margie was pleased that you brought up the conversation. I'm really glad you asked me to help you. The first few times we spoke I wasn't really there to help you. I should have been more open. I'm afraid I was wrapped up in my own problems," he said.

"Oh, no," Sarah started to protest, but Ed interrupted her.

"It's true, and I'm not normally like that. I'd like to tell you something."

"You don't have to explain."

54

"I want to," Ed said, "I don't know if you've heard, but I moved here following my divorce."

"I'm sorry. I didn't know. I thought you were married."

"Yes," he said, looking down at his ring, "I can't get up the courage to remove it. It's just that it has been a really difficult time for me. It wasn't that I didn't want to talk to you. I was finding it difficult, to make new friends, be in a new town and a new job, all that."

"I feel silly now. I guess I was avoiding talking to you too!"

"Why?" Ed said, laughing.

"Well," Sarah said, "I didn't want to give the wrong impression. Me being a young single woman, I need to keep a professional demeanor."

"I think we should start a club called People Who Give The Wrong First Impressions," Ed said, grinning.

"I think we would be flooded with members."

"Well, I'm glad to hear it went well with Margie, and I'm always here if you need any help with the planning or the feedback."

"Thanks again," Sarah said and walked back to her classroom. At the end of the afternoon, as she did every day, Sarah made notes of anything she had noticed in particular. This helped her to identify any possible areas of improvement and plan future lessons. Now she would also use these notes to prepare her feedback for Margie. Sarah marked this day on her planner with a big circle and an exclamation mark. A very good day indeed! This felt like her first day at Jackson Elementary School. The future was wide open.

Reflection

It was odd. After meeting Mr. Coles almost every week in the parking lot before, now that Sarah actually wanted to run into him he was nowhere to be seen. Everybody was getting busier as the Christmas break was approaching. She didn't want to stalk him at the parking lot so she walked up to his office at the end of the week.

"Come in!" he called out.

"Hello, Mr. Coles," "Sorry to interrupt you."

The principal was looking intently at his computer. He stopped typing and turned to the door.

"Sarah! How nice to see you. How is everything going?"

"Great," said Sarah, "I just wanted to thank you for the report you gave me. It really made a difference."

"I'm glad to hear that, because I wrote it!"

"Really?"

"But the credit goes to my mentor. I just expanded on what he started."

"Well, it is very good," Sarah said, "in fact I've had some results already."

"It is so important to communicate meaning, isn't it, and yet it is so easy to forget this. As our world becomes more rushed we tend to exchange sound bites."

"Exactly. I thought I knew this but being in a new environment created a new set of challenges for me."

"Naturally. We never really know how we are going to react to a new situation. We can prepare and train for a new voyage but that doesn't mean that we won't hit some bumps along the way. Which reminds me. I made a note here that you wished to have a meeting with me; there was something you wanted to discuss. Would you like to do that now? Or we can schedule a meeting for next week, if you prefer?"

Sarah thought back to that day just before Thanksgiving. She had meant to present her resignation as soon as she got back from her trip home. That seemed like such a long time ago now, as if it had happened to a different person.

"That won't be necessary," Sarah said, "I think that report you wrote pretty much sorted it out for me."

"Are you sure? I have time now if there is anything you need to talk about."

"I'm good. Everything's really good. I just stopped by to thank you for the report."

"Well, you can bring any concerns to our midyear meeting, but let me know if you need to schedule something before that, and I'll be seeing you at the team meetings of course."

"I'll see you there. Thanks again and have a great weekend."

As Sarah turned to leave, Mr. Coles called her back.

"Sarah!" Mr. Coles said, biting his upper lip as he stared at the computer screen, "maybe you can help me with something."

"Sure," what is it?"

"I need a theme for the next newsletter. I'm thinking something about communication. Since you just read the report you may have it fresh in your mind. If you had to write one sentence to sum up quality conversations what would it be?

Sarah thought for a moment and then replied, "Mean what you say and say what you mean."

"Perfect!" Mr. Coles declared, typing away on his keyboard, "I couldn't have said it better myself."

Part 2:
The Implementation

The Walk-Through

With the lessening of stress at work, Sarah found herself enjoying her free time more than before. She noticed that her sense of wellbeing reflected outwards and attracted others to approach her and invite her to join in. She had been putting off joining a book club that met every first Thursday of the month to discuss the classics. Her friend Amberlee, who had graduated a year ahead of her in college, kept inviting Sarah, knowing of her love for literature, but Sarah never seemed to find the time. This week was Amberlee's turn to host the group in her home and Sarah decided it would be a good time to give it a try. They were discussing a book she was very familiar with, *The Good Earth* by Pearl Buck. Armed with a tray of homemade asparagus tartlets and a bottle of sparkling cider, Sarah headed over to Amberlee's. On the way there, she thought how Amy and Ed might enjoy the book club as well. Was it a good idea to mix socializing and work colleagues or should she keep the two separate? It might be better to let Amy take the lead. If she invited Sarah for something outside work, then Sarah would reciprocate. She could also ask Amberlee for her opinion. It would be interesting to see if any of Amberlee's colleagues were included this evening. Amberlee taught in a school not far from Jackson. Sarah couldn't remember the name. It wasn't on the same level as Jackson, that's for sure.

Amberlee hugged Sarah and welcomed her into her townhouse. Sarah noticed that her cheeks looked a little paler than usual, or maybe her hair made it look like it. She had dyed it a shade of red brighter than her natural auburn color, and there was a puffiness under her watery grey eyes, as if she had been crying. But she was smiling and took Sarah's trays and led her into the kitchen. Everything was gleaming and tidy; it gave it the air of one of those model homes in a new condominium development.

Amberlee asked Sarah to help her spread the smoked salmon and dill pâté on tiny melba toasts while she fussed back and forth setting everything down on the wide low table in the seating area. With the table filled with the food and crystal glasses, the room suddenly felt more welcoming and Sarah started to feel more at ease. As soon as the guests arrived the room filled with color, conversation, and laughter and the difference from the sterile feeling that she had felt in the beginning was remarkable.

Sarah thought that this evening was a perfect metaphor for a quality conversation. Just as all the food and drinks were prepared and ready to be served, information is ready and waiting to be shared, whether it's from books, articles, or the web. And just as guests had been invited to partake, people need to be invited to share in the conversation to help information really come alive. A party's not a party if the food stays in the fridge and the guests all stay at home! Sarah felt inspired to share her newfound knowledge of quality conversations and get the party started!

"What do you think, Sarah? Are the internet and electronic books really going to be the end of traditional books as we know them?" one of the male guests asked.

"That would be too awful to consider," said Amberlee with a flourish, before Sarah could reply, "books give me such infinite pleasure."

"I don't think so," Sarah said, "I think the internet could be quite complementary. You can join in discussions about what you've just read, get recommendations and suggestions for other books, be up to date on upcoming publications, book tours by the authors, and so much more. The tangible book in the traditional format is what we need to feel in our hands, to flip through casually or get immersed in, to have at the bedside table, in our tote bags, take on vacation with us, and curl up with it on a rainy afternoon. I think it will be just like movie theatres; it is a different experience to see a film together with a group of people on a big screen, with big sound. We also enjoy watching movies at home. They both have their place." "Well said! I agree with you, the internet is a great place for information and exchange. This group was coordinated online. We got connected for this book club through meetup.com."

Amberlee rearranged the platter on the table, interrupting the exchange between Sarah and the young man. Sarah could see Amberlee was really into this guy. She wanted to ask Amberlee about him later, and also ask why she had been crying, but Sarah didn't know her so well, and these questions could be misinterpreted as prying. The conversation had now turned to the book , and the moment passed. Sarah helped Amberlee clear the table and bring out desserts. There were brownies and store-bought raspberry squares that were surprisingly rubbery, in spite of their picture-perfect glistening tops. As the group started to thin out, Sarah observed that the young man, whom she now knew was called Tom and worked as a management consultant in the city, was the last to leave.

He followed her into the kitchen several times to help clear the table, but she quickly refused any help and joined Amberlee back in the living room. She didn't want to give the appearance of getting between Amberlee and him, but he certainly was not making things any easier. Sarah wished he would direct his attention to Amberlee, where it would be welcomed. In different circumstances Sarah would have been flattered; he was charming and attractive, but tonight the timing was off. When everybody finally left, Sarah helped Amberlee do the washing up and they had a chance to talk, but Sarah's efforts at conversation were falling flat.

"I was wondering on the way here if there would be any of your coworkers in the club. Do you work with any of them?"

"No." Amberlee turned to face the sink, with her back to the room.

"They were all so nice," Sarah said.

"They are great."

Sarah decided to push a little further.

"Particularly Tom," Sarah said, "wasn't he friendly?"

"He seemed to like you."

"Hardly," Sarah said, lying, "he was looking at you all night."

"No he wasn't. He kept following you into the kitchen."

"Do you like him?"

"Maybe." Amberlee said, but Sarah could tell she was not going to open up easily.

"Have you known him long?"

"No."

Sarah decided she'd get further with Amberlee by asking her an open question that left her no choice but to volunteer more information. "So what's the story with Tom?" she asked.

Amberlee turned off the faucet and swung around, leaning against the sink.

"Well," Amberlee started, "I met him a couple of months ago, through the book club. He's just coming out of a long-term relationship. His fiancée apparently called off the wedding through a brutal text message. Can you believe it? Behaved quite appallingly but I don't know the details. He was heartbroken, but he's on the mend now. He's a management consultant in the city, but you know that. Right after my first book club meeting he asked me out for coffee. He had my email address through the group. It was very nice. We talked about books and me being new to the town. He recommended nice places to eat and to visit. I thought we had a great time, but now I am not sure if it was a date or not, because he never asked me out again."

"Why don't you ask him?"

"Are you insane?" Amberlee said, laughing, "it would sound desperate."

"I don't mean in that way, but maybe you can find a way to ask without getting personal?"

"Oh yeah? How?"

"I would need to know him better. Can you tell me more about him?" Sarah asked, hoping another open question would help Amber continue to share.

Amberlee swiveled a kitchen chair around and sat on it backwards .

"He likes to cook. Tom's dream is to one day open his own bistro; he is saving up for it and taking cooking lessons on the weekends. He seemed so passionate about it, and he kept asking if he was boring me with his stories, but the truth was that I was fascinated. I have always had an interest in food, although I never had a chance to really learn to cook, because my mom's such a good cook and then in college I survived on Ramen noodles and nachos. I could have listened to him all night. Did you hear how interesting his conversation was? He listens to other people; he is genuinely interested in what you have to say. He is so amazing. Tom is so gentle and kind, maybe that's why his fiancée took advantage of him. Why do good men choose cold-hearted women? Is it the pursuit of some universal balance? Kind with unkind; yin with yang? Oh well, I guess if he's not interested in me there is no point in pushing the subject any further. Maybe he's not ready to date yet. His loss."

"Maybe he just need a little more time," Sarah said, "you'll keep seeing each other at the book meetings."

"True," Amberlee replied, "Who knows? Anything is possible, but I am not holding my breath. He'll have to make it clear if he's asking me on a date or not next time, if there is a next time."

At this point Amberlee looked completely relaxed; she paused for a long time and was now absently playing with her fingers on the leftover raspberry squares.

"Those things were awful," she said, cracking a smile.

"Yes, they were," Sarah hesitated, laughing as she said, "not great...."

"I paid a fortune at a fancy bakery downtown, just to impress Tom," Amberlee started giggling, "and they tasted like a PVC pipe!"

"How would you know? When was the last time you had a PVC pipe for dessert?" They both giggled like schoolgirls.

"I bet Tom was really impressed with my gourmet choices." Amberlee gasped for air with tears spilling down her cheeks.

The rest of the evening went by easily with both of them sprawled on the carpet, chatting and listening to old records, talking about everything and nothing. Finally, when it was getting late, Sarah picked up her handbag and as she rifled through it for her car keys, she casually brought up the question she had meant to ask all evening.

"Amberlee," she said, "I meant to ask you earlier, but I didn't want to pry."

"You noticed I had been crying? I was hoping it wouldn't show."

Sarah shrugged her shoulders gently.

"Just some problems at work. I didn't want to talk about it because it is not for sure yet, but there is a possibility that I may have to transfer out of my school."

"Really? What's wrong?"

"They may have to reduce some staff," she said, "consolidate classes. But there is nothing certain yet, and we don't know who would be affected, but being one of the newest I'd expect it would probably be me."

"I'm so sorry to hear that," Sarah said, "do you know where you'd be going?"

"Not really," she said, "besides, there's so many different versions and gossip going around that I don't know what to believe. I'll just put it out of my mind. I was just feeling sorry for myself today. I feel like I was just beginning to settle in this townhouse. It was starting to feel like home, and if I have to move again..."

"Like you said," Sarah said," It's better not to worry about it until you have more information. Is there anybody you could ask?"

"The principal," Amberlee said, "she's been really supportive, but I fear that her job may be at stake too. The board is not happy and they may look for a scapegoat. It's all very confusing."

"If there is anything I can do," Sarah said.

"Of course," Amberlee said, "actually, you've helped me tremendously today. I had a great time and now I'm so tired I'm sure I'll get a good night's sleep."

When they hugged good-bye Amberlee was smiling, but Sarah left with mixed feelings. During the short drive back home she felt light with the pleasure of the relaxing time

70

she had spent with Amberlee and the stimulating conversation of the book club, because she had been able to disconnect from her own worries about her career and Jackson. At the same time, she felt a heavy heart for Amberlee and hoped that things would resolve themselves at her school and that she wouldn't be forced to uproot herself from either job or home anytime soon. She made a mental note to call Amberlee soon to see how she was doing.

The teachers who were good at communication had no problem talking to Sarah about her newfound enthusiasm for quality conversations. In the lounge, before and after grade-level meetings, she was gathering other people's impressions on the four pillars of quality conversation. Amy, for example, was a natural communicator. That next Monday during a break Sarah was flipping through a magazine in the lounge and noticed an article on asking open questions. When Amy arrived, Sarah waved her over and showed her the article.

"I know," Amy said, "open questions. It's so simple, isn't it?"

Ed approached them and they showed him the article.

"Hmm," he said, "I don't know. Sounds too easy to be true."

"But it works!" Sarah said, "Just last week, a friend of mine and I were having a bit of a challenging conversation and I started asking open questions and it all turned around."

71

Two other teachers had now joined the conversation and were looking over the article.

"People get defensive if you ask questions that could feel like you're prying," said the other.

"That's exactly the point," Sarah said, "the principle is to ask questions, the right question at the right time, depending on the information that is required to move the conversation forward. If all you need to know is the time, then that is the appropriate question. When you match the question to the conversation, you have quality, but if you settle for matching the conversation to the question, you gradually add noise instead of information until you end up losing the thread of the conversation. Without revealing any details, Sarah related the difference that open questions had made in her conversation with Amberlee.

Amy supported Sarah's explanation and Ed joined in until it was time to get back to work.

"You know, Sarah," one of the other teachers said, "I was skeptical but once I heard your explanation, I thought you said some very interesting things. I think I'll try this quality conversation business with my husband next time we decide where we want to go on vacation… that will be the real test of the four pillars."

They all laughed.

"But seriously, it's a shame we don't talk about this in our meetings," the other said, "This could be such a useful subject."

"I would definitely want to know more about this," Ed added, "maybe we could suggest it to Margie?"

Sarah looked down at her shoes. She didn't want to be difficult, but at the mention of Margie she instinctively withdrew. Although she was feeling more and more comfortable in their meetings and getting a much better grip of what she thought of as the backstage aspects of her teaching job, she didn't know that she was ready to volunteer and stick her neck out yet.

"That's a good idea," Amy said, "I bet Margie will be receptive. Maybe even discuss it with Mr. Coles."

This was getting out of hand. Sarah had meant for it to be a casual conversation with some colleagues during a break, and now it was taking on a life of its own. It was one thing to believe that quality conversations were important; it was quite another to be seen as a junior member of the school to be imposing her ideas on other more experienced and seasoned professionals. This was more of a commitment than she felt inclined to make. And yet she didn't want to shy away from the challenge.

If there were to be people sharing at the quality conversations table, it seemed that it was up to Sarah to send out the invitation. As the newest member of the team, she knew that she would be under scrutiny, so she had to get it right the first time.

"Let me think about it," Sarah said, "I feel I need to be more prepared. I am still learning about all this myself."

"Sounds good," Amy said, "besides, with the Christmas pageant and the Christmas rush it's probably not the best time to bring anything new right now."

"Maybe we can talk about it after the Christmas break," Sarah said.

With that in mind, the trip back home to her family over Christmas seemed even more purposeful. She would have some time to reflect, get organized, and prepare her pitch to Margie. She kept a copy of the article and put it together with the paper from Mr. Coles and her notes about the conversation with Noah and with Amberlee. She had now gotten into the habit of writing down anything that helped her refine the ideas of the four pillars, or any snippets she heard on the radio, on TV, or from her own conversations which would help illustrate them. Her file was quickly thickening.

That afternoon when she got home, there was a message from Amberlee. She said she had some news she'd like to share and asked if Sarah would join her for pizza that evening at Salute. She had heard of the place; it was an Italian restaurant run on purely organic principles with mostly locally sourced ingredients. The restaurant was connected with a bookstore that regularly held authors' book signings and workshops. It had become very fashionable but she had never had a chance to visit , so she was excited about it and curious about what the news would be. Maybe Tom had asked Amberlee out after all? Sarah called her back immediately, and they arranged to meet , although Amberlee would not give Sarah any indication of what the news was about.

"You'll have to wait and see!" she said, laughing and then hanging up. At least it sounded like it was good news. The place was buzzing with people. Salute had an air of Spartan simplicity that belied a highly refined attention to detail. The solid oak tables were covered with starched

74

white linen tablecloths; and the polished hardwood floors, plain white walls, and brushed steel light fixtures were reminiscent of an art gallery. Although instead of works of art, the focus of the eye in this space was drawn to the people themselves.

Against such an unassuming background, the bright colors of the dresses, the hair, and the makeup, highlighted the people inside. One of the walls opened through a wide archway into the bookstore, and there the white walls and oak shelving continued, but the objects of focus were the books in their multicolored slots competing for the customer's attention.

To Sarah, a row of books held an irresistible allure; all those ideas and experiences were waiting to pull her in and transport her to different worlds. To other people it would be the temptation of the department store with beautiful shoes and handbags, or maybe leafing through brochures for a vacation on an exotic beach. To Sarah, the ultimate luxury of passing time was to become immersed in books. A bookstore such as this had a gravitational pull for her. Sarah found Amberlee already sitting at their table looking at the menu. Mere minutes after they placed their order, their two individual whole-grain pizzas arrived, spinach and gorgonzola for Amberlee and taleggio cheese, cherry tomatoes, and arugula for Sarah.

"This is delicious," Sarah said, "I'm glad you picked this place."

"I've been wanting to come since Tom recommended it," Amberlee replied, biting into her pizza, "it's his favorite. Apparently his office is near here."

Sarah instinctively scanned the room to see if Tom just happened to be there.

"Please don't tell me that we are here just in the hope that we'll run into him?" Sarah said. She was only half-joking; she didn't know Amberlee that well.

"Honestly, Sarah," Amberlee said, comically rolling her eyes, then smiling, "it's just that he raved about the food here."

"Well," Sarah said, "Tom was right, so now we know he has good taste in pizza, among his many other attributes. So what's the reason we are here then?"

"It turns out that the rumors at work were true," Amberlee said, "I'm getting transferred."

Sarah swallowed hard. She was confused. It wasn't good news after all. Why did she seem so upbeat then?

"I'm so sorry," "do you know where to?"

"Jackson!" Amberlee said, and paused to see Sarah's reaction.

A moment passed before the information sunk in.

"My Jackson?"

"Isn't that fantastic?" Amberlee said, speaking quickly now, "it just fits so perfectly. It is near my home, I won't have to move, you are there so I already have a friend. Not to mention, it is a much more prestigious school than the one I was at, which is going through a rather shaky restructuring, so it is like getting a promotion! I'm so excited."

Sarah shook herself and thought: *Amberlee at Jackson? My school, where I am just now carving out a place for myself?* For some reason the news was not provoking the welcoming reaction that Amberlee would be expecting. She tried her best to feel happy for Amberlee.

"What are the odds?" Sarah said, wishing she had a better choice of words, "I mean, of all the schools in the city, it is such a coincidence."

"Not entirely coincidental," Amberlee said, "you know that movie *Six Degrees of Separation*?"

"Doesn't it talk about how any person on earth can be connected to any other person by at least five other people through circles of acquaintances."

"Pretty much, yes," Amberlee said, "the principal of my school goes to the same church as the principal of your school, Mr. Coles."

"Aha." Sarah was beginning to dislike the story more and more.

"So naturally, when this came up in conversation, I kept my antenna up for any possibility of a position at Jackson and started going to that church. It is not much farther than mine anyway, so I met Mr. Coles and mentioned that I had a college best friend who worked at Jackson."

Sarah thought that to call them best friends was stretching the truth somehow, but Amberlee may have meant it as a compliment, so she let it go.

"Anyway," Amberlee said, "long story short, apparently things accelerated and they were forced to make the transfers much faster than anticipated, and maybe the fact that Mr. Coles already knew me helped."

Sarah had to admire Amberlee's determination, although she wasn't quite sure that the theory of six degrees applied; it sounded more like a case of using any

77

means to an end. The fact that her name had been brought up without her knowledge was not sitting well either, but she decided to give her friend the benefit of the doubt. It would be easy for Sarah to judge; it was not her job at stake, so she tried to put herself in Amberlee's shoes. At the same time, however, she did not entirely approve of the methods and she decided that in this case she would listen but would not ask any further questions. She wasn't sure that she really wanted to know more.

"So when do you start?" Sarah asked.

"After the Christmas break," Amberlee said, "by the way, I'm not supposed to say anything until your principal announces it, but I already know I'm not on your same grade-level, which is a good thing so I won't have that horrid Margie as my grade-level chair."

Sarah now wished she had not discussed her initial misgivings with Margie in such an open way, although at the time she had mentioned it to Amberlee in a casual email she could hardly foresee that her college roommate would end up working in the same school, and she had been in a state of emotional turmoil.

"Margie is actually really nice," Sarah said, "I just had not really communicated with her at the level of a quality conversation."

"Don't worry." Amberlee patted Sarah's hand across the table. "I deleted your email, and I won't tell her what you said."

Sarah wasn't quite sure how to take that comment. In any case, she had never said anything against Margie personally; she had just referred to her own trouble understanding what the expectations about her job were.

"Really, I have a better understanding of Margie. I have been using some quality conversation pillars that are really amazing."

"What pillars?" Amberlee said.

Sarah was relieved to change the subject away from the school and Margie, and she launched into a description of the four pillars with examples, finally coming to her own conversation with Amberlee the day of the book club party.

"So I was one of your experiments?" Amberlee asked, eyes open wide." Not at all," Sarah said, "it just happened that way, and I realized that the four pillars were working."

"Well, then I expect I'll be mentioned in the acknowledgements when you write your book."

"There's no book," Sarah said, laughing, "it's just a simple practice that actually works."

"Right," said Amberlee, "it's actually too simple. You are not going to tell me that all the communication problems in the world can be solved by using four pillars. It's not realistic. Otherwise you should call the White House and tell them that you know the solution to the peace effort in the Middle East, and then sit back and listen to the laughter."

Sarah didn't reply; she pretended to be concentrating on her pizza, although it had already gone cold by that time.

"Look," Amberlee said, "I'm sorry, I didn't mean to rain on your parade like that. Forget what I just said. Actually, I say more power to you. You've found something you obviously feel passionate about, and if it makes you feel like you could actually improve things, even a little bit,

79

even if only for a few people, then it's worth doing. This deserves a toast. Here's to quality conversations!"

Sarah raised her glass to meet Amberlee's and forced a smile. If she couldn't even persuade her friend to take her seriously, what chance did she have with Margie or Mr. Coles? Maybe Amberlee was right; maybe she was Don Quixote against the windmills, and there was a good reason why Mr. Coles's report about the four pillars was not more widely incorporated into practical application in real life. Both Amy and Margie had read the report before, and they hadn't suddenly become evangelists for the four pillars, so why did she, a newbie, think that she would make a difference?

"Maybe I am a bit optimistic," Sarah said, "and I've been wearing rose-colored glasses, but I can honestly say that it worked for me."

"Of course it did," Amberlee said, "and that's what counts, isn't it? The proof is in the doing."

"But I can get a little carried away sometimes," Sarah said, "I've been a little obsessed with this lately, reading everything I can get my hands on. Maybe I'm overdoing it."

"It's hard to tell if it's genuine enthusiasm or obsession if you don't have someone to bounce ideas off of."

Sarah considered for a moment. *Was she creating an island unto herself?* She had discussed these ideas with a few people, but it was also possible that just because she wanted the pillars to work, she was creating a bubble where they had an effect. Perhaps, she was not taking into consideration that most conversations take place when people are distracted, stressed, rushed, or simply uninterested.

80

Maybe having someone to discuss ideas with was a way to keep from getting carried away. On impulse, she looked at Amberlee with fresh purpose. Had she been placed in her path to be a balance to her exuberance?

"Amberlee," she said, "I have an idea. Now that we will be working together, I think we should become critical peers."

"That sounds important," Amberlee said, "what does it involve?"

"Mostly we would seek to develop each other's professional and leadership skills," Sarah explained, "we would get together regularly and support each other's goals and achievements and be critical if needed. We would give each other feedback and help keep our efforts in balance."

"I'm in," Amberlee said, "let's meet here for pizza every two weeks. So we'll be away from the school. You know, it's our neutral ground."

"And the fact that the pizza is fantastic doesn't hurt," Sarah said, and batted her eyelashes, "and that maybe we might run into a certain management consultant who likes gourmet food? No seriously, meeting here sounds fine, and if something comes up in between and we don't want to wait then we can always have an AD hoc short meeting or phone call."

"You've got a deal," Amberlee said, "I think this momentous occasion deserves a really sinful dessert. You pick."

"How about this one, panna cota with mango sauce," Sarah said.

As the dessert arrived followed by herbal tea with little amaretti cookies, they both reinforced their commitment to help each other in the development of their skills.

81

They split the check and Amberlee quickly hugged Sarah goodbye and stepped back outside , but Sarah's steps led her in the opposite direction, through the archway to the bookstore next door.

The first thing she noticed was the smell. There was absolutely no hint of food although it was right next to the restaurant; the air was scented with the familiar smell of leather and ink, a combination she found familiar and relaxing. She ambled slowly past rows and rows of titles, beyond the bestselling novels and motivational books on to the less glittery non-fiction sections. Somebody had left a book on a table that caught her eye. It was simply called *Conversations*, and there were no jazzy graphics on the cover—just the title. Sarah settled on a quiet bench to leaf through it. She was immediately pulled in. Right there, in the first few pages, were examples of the four pillars at work, story after story of people who had used the technique and who had made a breakthrough in their communications either at work or in their personal lives. She didn't need to look any further. Although it would blow her budget for tonight, she decided to buy the book. It would be her Christmas present to herself.

That evening, as she was getting ready for bed, Sarah thought back at her impulse of asking Amberlee to be her critical peer and felt a pang of doubt. She looked in the mirror, while she vigorously brushed her teeth.

"Did you just do a stupid thing tonight?" she asked her reflection, with her mouth full of foam, "What do you think?"

82

Great, she thought, *now I'm talking to myself.* She tried to shake the cynical feeling that Amberlee may not have been the right choice of critical peer, since she didn't seem to share some of her values. She was tired; she would be more clear-headed in the morning. She always did her best thinking in the mornings, so she gratefully slid into bed and into the new world of her book *Conversations*.

The next thing Sarah saw was the blinking red numbers on her alarm clock at 7:05 a.m. *What?* She took a sharp breath. Had she slept through the alarm? How was she going to get ready and get to school in time? She stumbled into the shower, and as she toweled off a needling pain shot inside her ears making her let out a moan. Hoping it was not an infection, she rifled through her kitchen drawer for a pain reliever when the phone rang. It was Gayle.

"Sarah!" her little sister cried.

"Gayle, what's wrong?"

"It's awful. Dad's been taken to hospital."

"What happened? Is he all right?" Sarah felt her throat tighten.

"He had a restless night, couldn't sleep well, and Mom said he went all white and clutched both hands to his chest in pain."

"Oh my goodness, Gayle," Sarah felt another sharp pang in her ears. "I'll come home."

"No, Sarah," Gayle said, "you have to work. I'm doing OK and Noah is taking care of the farm. They're going to run some tests."

83

"Are you sure?"

"Yes, I'm sure," Gayle said, calmer now, "maybe you could come down over the weekend?"

"I'll be there Friday evening."

"Great, Sis," Gayle said, "you know, I've never seen Dad sick before, he seemed so…"

"What?"

"Human," Gayle said, "just like any of us."

"He *is* human, Gayle,"

"Not to me, he isn't," Gayle said, her voice trembling again, "he's made of solid gold to me, Sis. I don't know what I'd do without him."

"He'll be all right," Sarah said, as much for her own sake as for Gayle's comfort. "Listen, I'm already late for work. I'll call you back this afternoon."

"Sure," Gayle said, "sorry to dump on you like this."

Sarah felt twice as bad for not being able to listen to her sister at this stressful time. She swallowed the pain reliever left her hair wet, and jumped in her car before her brain had come to terms with the fact that it was a new day.

She parked and rushed through the already empty corridors, hoping that nobody would notice her wet hair tied tightly into a ponytail, the absence of makeup, and the slightly creased skirt that had not quite made it to the dry cleaners yet. Sarah couldn't recall a time when she left the house in such a state, not even when she was on vacation or helping on the farm.

Adjusting to a new routine was a challenge for anyone, let alone adjusting to a brand new career as well. *Staying up late last night was not such a brilliant idea,* Sarah

84

thought. *I need to find a way to balance some social life into my schedule, without disrupting my work. Who am I kidding? Staying up past midnight reading?* Her stomach grumbled, because of the non-existing breakfast.

She trotted past Mr. Coles' office just as he was ushering in a man and a woman dressed in expensive suits, something you would expect to see in the lobby of a big city law firm. As they turned to enter the office Sarah caught a glimpse of their faces and recognized them as the parents of one of her students. In her hurried state, she strained to recall if she had been notified of any request for a meeting by these parents. Had they some concern about her that they felt obliged to go directly to Mr. Coles's office? Wouldn't Mr. Coles have notified her if that were the case? Should she make herself available for the meeting? Certainly not; if Mr. Coles hadn't asked her to attend, that would be inappropriate.

Could there be a complaint about her performance as a teacher? Already? If so, then Mr. Coles would inform her in due time. She wondered if she should mention it to him or to wait until he brought it up. After all, if she hadn't happened to see the parents walking into his office right now she would never had known about their meeting. She lingered for a moment across from Mr. Coles's office but quickly decided to keep moving. In any case, there was nothing she could do about it right now. Mr. Coles would have good reason to complain the she didn't show up ready for work on time, so she went directly to her classroom. A teaching assistant was sitting in for her just as the children were settling in their desks. She was

85

late. She thanked the assistant and gathered her breath. A few moments later, Margie popped her head in through the door. Sarah went up to meet her.

"Good morning, Sarah," Margie said, her hair and makeup impeccably put together as always, "I didn't see you in the lounge."

"Good morning Margie," Sarah said, "I came in straight to the classroom."

"Is everything OK?" Margie said.

"Yes, fine," Sarah said, repeatedly smoothing her skirt.

"Good," Margie said, "just thought I'd mention that the grade-level meeting got pushed back half an hour. I circulated a memo but wanted to mention it in person. Hope it doesn't interfere with your schedule."

"Sure," Sarah said, "no problem."

"Wonderful," Margie said, "I'm looking forward to your proposal for the after-school program."

Sarah's smile froze as Margie disappeared as quickly as she had arrived. After-school program? What? Not another item she had missed from the orange folder? How was this possible? The orange folder was taking on almost mythical proportions. After acing all those classes in college, being the star of the teacher-training class, most likely to succeed and all that...for this? Could this day get any more surreal?

Sarah found it hard to shake the grip of the early morning mishaps. She couldn't stop thinking about her Dad in the hospital, she still hadn't had any breakfast, her hair was a flat shapeless mat and her confidence wasn't much better, and she kept remembering her conversation with Amberlee about becoming critical peers. She won-

86

dered if Amberlee's transfer would be announced today. Her mind was racing but a few minutes into her class, her training kicked in and she was again in the flow of her lesson, enjoying the students, bouncing off their natural energy and enthusiasm. When it was time for lunch, Sarah headed for the phones to call her mother. To her surprise, it was her father who answered the phone.

"Dad!" Sarah said, "I thought you'd still be at the hospital."

"I escaped through the window," he said, back to his jovial self.

"Seriously, Dad, what happened?" Sarah asked.

"Oh, nothing, you know how your Mum likes to make things dramatic," he said.

But Sarah knew better.

"Come on, Dad. Mom said you had chest pains." Sarah heard a click on the line meaning that her Mom was on the other phone.

"Yes he did," her Mom said, "he looked white as a sheet and couldn't tell me what was wrong. He gave me the scare of my life, Sarah."

"So what did the doctors say?"

"Your dad has acid reflux!" her Mom said, barely containing a chuckle.

"They said it might be that," her Dad said, "they didn't say for sure."

"In any case, Dad, I'm so happy to hear it was that and not something worse."

"I'm a tough old ox," he said, "I don't know what the fuss is about. Anyway, I'll let you talk to your Mom," he paused, "I love you, kid."

87

The words never sounded sweeter to Sarah.

"Gayle said you were coming down on the weekend," her mother said, "not necessary, honey. We'll see you at Christmas in just a few days. Dad is fine. It's just a matter of watching his diet. He has developed this annoying habit of snacking just before going to bed and the snacks gradually got bigger and bigger over time. Then he goes straight to sleep so he doesn't have time to digest. Plus we all overdid it on Thanksgiving, didn't we?"

"We sure did. I couldn't zip up my jeans the next day."

"So how are things at work," her mom said, "any improvement?"

"Actually, yes," Sarah said, "some colleagues of mine are helping me. They are really nice and one of them, Amy, used to teach 4th grade, so she has experience with the same material."

"That sounds good."

"I just heard that Amberlee from college is transferring to my school," Sarah said.

"Really? That's so nice, to have a friend there," her mom said.

"Sure," Sarah said, unconvinced, and quickly changed the subject," I have been reading up on some interesting subjects, like how to have better conversations. I think I am beginning to understand what I can improve."

"I'm so pleased to hear it, Sarah. It made me so sad that you wanted to quit. You said you wanted to be a teacher when you were in the fourth grade yourself. That day at dinner, you sat down so serious and determined and announced that you were going to be a teacher, just like Mrs. Lee."

"I remember," Sarah said, smiling, "I remember that day very well."

Mrs. Lee had been her favorite teacher. She hadn't thought about Mrs. Lee for a long time. *I wonder how she is doing. She must be retired by now.*

After talking to her family Sarah went out for a walk and let the wave of relief sweep through her. She felt grateful, for the doctors at the hospital, for her colleagues at work, for her family, for having a job she loved, and for the earache that had disappeared. Sarah grabbed Margie's orange folder and her notepad, where she had been scribbling notes from the book the night before, and looked for the references to the after-school program. She found it right away, being more familiar with the contents after Margie's explanation. She quickly identified the initiative. What could she contribute? Her eyes went to her notepad with the notes on quality conversations. Then she thought back to Ed and Amy suggesting that she bring up the topic of quality conversations in the grade-level meetings. But what about making it an after-school program? Could it work? How to structure it? Who would participate? Who would lead it? How to monitor results? Oh, well, it would have to wait. She had more urgent things to take care of right now, such as getting something to eat before her knees buckled under her.

Margie started the grade-level meeting as the last few participants were arriving.

"First of all let me say that I appreciate your flexibility with the schedule change," Margie said, "next meeting will go back to the normal time. I'll try to keep everything short today so that we can all get back to our last-minute Christmas shopping."

The group laughed and Sarah noticed out of the corner of her eye that Mr. Coles was in the corridor.

"I have an announcement before we start," Margie glanced up at Sarah, , then looked back at her notes, "we will have a new member of staff joining us after the Christmas break, Amberlee Gray, in the fifth grade. Mr. Coles will be making the announcement later but I just wanted to give you a heads up and as always I'm sure you'll make her feel welcome. We all know it is a little harder to settle when the school year is already under way, but I believe she has a friend in here already."

Margie looked up at Sarah again.

"I know Amberlee," Sarah said, all eyes on her, "from college."

Now everyone would link Amberlee with Sarah, so whatever impression they got from the newcomer would also reflect on her. It was in these unsaid messages that most impressions are firmly fixed. Sarah accepted that Amberlee had just become her tacit protégé. Margie then worked her way through the first two items of the day and finally got to the after-school programs. The chess club was losing membership, and the "Healthy Groove" program that taught children about health and nutrition was doing well.

"So I would like to hear from you any ideas for future after-school programs that we could consider, as the chess seems to have run its course. Apparently kids are now playing chess online. Anyway, any ideas? How about you, Sarah?"

90

There seemed to be no way out of the spotlight today. She gathered her notes from her writing pad and drew a deep breath as if to jump off the side of a boat into the sea beyond.

"I have been doing some research on an area of interest, and there may be an idea for a program there, but I would need your help to give it shape."

The group looked to Sarah; some shuffled in their chairs. Brevity was the soul of wit, particularly when you were speaking to a room full of people itching to get on with their holidays chores. Just then the door opened and Mr. Coles entered the room quietly and took a seat in the back.

"Some of you may already be familiar with a paper that Mr. Coles has circulated with four pillars for quality conversations?" asked Sarah, acknowledging Mr. Coles with a small wave.

Most nodded their heads. Mr. Coles smiled.

"I have found these pillars very useful," Sarah continued, "I have applied them at work and in my private life, and I believe they would be very helpful to others."

A pause followed, as Sarah waited for comments or questions.

"Maybe you could refresh our memory as to what the pillars are," said Ed, helping her along.

"Sure, there are four pillars to a quality conversations. They are: listening, asking questions, giving and receiving feedback and, finally, reflection. There is much more to it than that, of course, and I am gathering experiences and examples, but I can already tell from experience that these four pillars work."

91

Margie was the first to pose a question.

"What leads you to think that this as an after-school program, rather than, say, a workshop or something to distribute in writing?"

"This information is not new. It is always available but somehow if we don't use it in an active way, we seem to forget it. We can strive to consistently say what we mean and mean what we say, but not many among us can say that we succeed most of the time. If we had a forum for discussion and exchange to remind us of the four pillars on a regular basis, I believe that *Quality Conversations* would come to life." Sarah remembered the impression she had from Amberlee's party. "It is like setting a table for a party. You can have the best food and beverages in the fridge and that could mean that there is the potential of having a party, but it is only when you actually invite people and set the table out for everyone to share that the party really happens. By taking an initiative you give the opportunity for the potential to become a reality."

Margie nodded assent, and Mr. Coles leaned forward in his chair.

"If I may," Ed said, "I already have an example in my personal life. I'll spare you the details but Sarah shared the four pillars with me and I applied it to a situation that, let's say, didn't have a lot of quality before. I noticed a huge improvement. I think this program could help many students."

Sarah looked at Ed with surprise. Could he be referring to his ex-wife? She had no idea that she had already helped someone. Ed had not mentioned it before. He

92

was obviously a very private person so she appreciated that he had offered this information to help her presentation today.

"Why stop with the students?" Mr. Coles voice rose from the back, making some of the group turn sideways to face him, "why not try to bring student, teachers, and parents together? We have never done a multi-level program before at Jackson, and it is about time that we do. We are always looked upon by other schools to lead the way. This could be a good experiment: The Quality Conversations After-School Program."

"Let's give it shape then," Margie said, looking back at Sarah, "do you think that you could have a proposal for us to jointly present to Mr. Coles after the Christmas break?"

Sarah felt her stomach tighten. This was it. Sink or swim.

"Absolutely," she heard herself say.

Later that afternoon, as Sarah was doing laundry and tidying up her apartment, she decided to have her first critical peer conversation with Amberlee. She wanted to bounce off her the idea of the after-school program.

"Hey Amberlee," Sarah said, "they announced your transfer today. It's official."

"Great," Amberlee said, "I can't wait to start. I wish I could go right now, so I could relax a bit more during the holidays. But I guess it makes sense to change after Christmas."

"Yes, it's only a couple of weeks away anyway,"

"You know what?" Amberlee said, "the lady who was hosting the book club meeting next month had to pull out. I thought of you. Would you like to do it?"

"Oh, I don't know," Sarah said, "I'm the newest member, would that be alright?"

"Of course," Amberlee said, "there's no better way to become part of the team. Jump straight in as a host."

"I guess it's all right. Do you think there's enough space in my apartment? It's kind of tiny."

"Of course," Amberlee said, "it will be nice and cozy. Besides, you make everyone feel welcome; you're a natural."

"Talking about jumping straight in the middle of things," said Sarah, "I wanted to touch base with you as a critical peer."

Sarah told Amberlee about the grade-level meeting and the possible initiative for the Quality Conversations after-school program. A long pause followed.

"Oh, Sarah, I don't know," Amberlee finally said, "it seems an awful lot to take on, being that it's your first year."

So much for jumping straight in! Sarah waited for the positive comment to balance out the first, but it didn't come.

"Besides," Amberlee continued, "you haven't really tried this "four pillar" thing with anyone in a formal environment, have you? It's just a theory at the moment. There's a lot riding on this theory. It's a bit flimsy, you know. I don't want you to get burned; it would be such a disappointment to fall flat on your face on your very first initiative. Couldn't you start with something smaller, more manageable? To take on parents, teachers, and students all in one go is a bit ambitious. I'm playing devil's advocate here."

"I appreciate it," Sarah said. "Don't think I haven't had the same thoughts myself. I have. But I truly believe in these four pillars. I know they work. But I hear what you're saying."

"Mind you, I am impressed that you have the courage to consider it," Amberlee said, "I don't know if I could."

Sarah made it an early night. The day had left her drained and exhausted, mostly from the scare with her father's health and then the mix of thrill and apprehension of the initiative for the after-school program. It had been a full day and she was grateful to take a hot bath and slide into bed.

The Experience

To Sarah's surprise, in the days following the grade team meeting not only Ed and Amy approached her to offer support, but a few teachers she hardly had the chance to talk to before were coming to her with suggestions and experiences. Most of them had read Mr. Coles paper about the four pillars and had their own ideas on how the practice of quality conversations could be brought to the parents and students. Sarah made notes and accepted all the suggestions. She didn't accept or reject them; she just collected them as if she was picking fruit in her orchard. Later on she would sort the ones that would stay and the ones that didn't fit. Over the holiday break she would have a chance to sort through all the ideas and notes and hopefully shape them into a coherent plan.

On the last day of school before the holidays, Mr. Coles stopped by Sarah's classroom.

"Sarah," he said, "you got a minute?"

"Of course," Sarah said, and motioned for him to take a seat.

Mr. Coles sat on the edge of her desk, with one leg dangling.

"I've noticed there is some excitement about your after-school program," said Mr. Coles.

"It's not mine," Sarah protested, "it's for all the school. It started with you, actually, with that paper."

"Oh, I did nothing," said Mr. Coles, "I just got that paper from someone else and copied it. But I had never turned the gears to put it into action; it is your initiative that may bring it to life more than anything I ever did."

Sarah didn't know what to say.

"I imagine that you may be a little hesitant to launch into this initiative," Mr. Coles said, "giving that just a few weeks ago you were having your own misgivings about being able to communicate effectively."

Sarah nodded.

"I want you to know," he continued, "that you have my full support, and that I am looking forward to your proposal. I brought you a list of resources that you may want to look up online, for support and maybe for ideas on how to structure the program."

With this, Mr. Coles handed her a two-page list of links to internet sites.

"Don't worry if you can't finish it in time," said Mr. Coles, "I wouldn't expect you to work over the holidays."

"I don't mind," Sarah said, "I find this very interesting; it hardly feels like work."

"That's what they say about choosing your vocation," Mr. Coles said, "find something you love and you won't have to work another day in your life. But I also want you to know that if you somehow find the time and you can submit it by the end of the holiday break, then we might be able to fit it in for this year. We could start right away. In fact, we have the resources available. We got a little boost in our budget by accepting a couple of last-minute transfers, such as your friend Amberlee. Anyway, no pressure, just something to consider."

"What do you mean when you say right away?" Sarah asked.

"Well, maybe end of January," Mr. Coles said. "One of our key indicators of performance at Jackson is student achievement. I have measured your class and we have noticed a slight increase. It could be just a blip or it could be the start of something remarkable. It is my job to give you the tools you need to try it and see if it's a blip or a real change. If you could bring this program to the whole school it would fit into those parameters. If we can bring quality conversations into the classroom, who knows what else we can achieve? I know this is a lot to digest in your first year, but it seems this is the way it is going. You may be meant for great things, Sarah, so you might as well buckle up and enjoy the ride!"

Mr. Coles rose and walked to the door, leaving a stunned Sarah to absorb his words.

"Merry Christmas!" Mr. Coles chimed, as he left.

Sarah mused over what Mr. Coles had just said. In her brief tenure at Jackson he had already noticed an improvement in her students. Sarah had made a conscious effort to bring quality conversations into her classroom, but she had never expected that it would make such a noticeable difference so soon. Things were really accelerating and she felt a mix of exhilaration and anxiety. Amberlee's words kept ringing in her ear "this is just a theory, it's a bit flimsy, it hasn't been tried yet." What had she let herself in for? Well, it was too late to pull out now. All she could do is try her best over the holidays and attempt not to stress about it. During the lunch break, Sarah approached Amy to tell her about her conversation with Mr. Coles.

"Guess what, Miss Quality Conversations?" Amy said, before Sarah could speak, "I am bringing the four pillars into the classroom. I've started with Active Listening today, and the kids are so interested. I haven't mentioned anything about the after-school program, of course, but to judge from the way they were paying attention today, it's going to be a big hit."

"Now you're scaring me," Sarah said, "it's all going so fast."

"There's nothing to worry about," Amy said, "just roll with it, Sarah. We are all supporting you. It's a great idea. It's engaging, it's fun, and it's real."

Ed joined in their conversation.

"Absolutely," he said, "we all need it, and the students may needed it now more than ever. With the internet, emails, texts, videogames, and social media they are increasingly skilled at electronic communications, but having a quality conversation may soon become a rare occurrence. These are skills that they will find useful for the rest of their lives. You can really make a difference here."

"For the parents too," added another teacher, "most households have parents out working all day, tired and stressed out, struggling with the way the kids seem to isolate themselves with their computers and their mobile phones. These ideas will give them practical tools to really talk to each other and make the best of the little time they have to enjoy each other's company."

Soon there was a circle of people all discussing the role that quality conversations play at home, at work, and even in the playground. Amy tugged at Sarah's sleeve and whispered in her ear.

"Look at what you've done," she whispered, "I've been here for a few years and I can't remember ever seeing such an animated conversation in the teacher's lounge."

It was becoming clear to Sarah that the four pillars of quality conversations had become her battle cry. Both positive and negative developments related to the planning and implementation of the after-school program would be automatically associated with her. What she was also learning is that the personal or professional triumphs or setbacks that her colleagues would experience in their own journeys through quality conversations would also be somehow linked to her. Things that were completely out of her control would be assigned to her name, pinned to her performance, and ultimately tagged onto her reputation as a teacher.

Whether she liked it or not, *Quality Conversations* had flickered into life thanks to her initiative, and it was up to her to fan the flame until it had enough power to continue on its own. There was no question in her mind that this was worth doing. The four pillars were solid; they worked. In order to be the champion of quality conversations she would have to make sure that she was living the four pillars in her own life. Was she really gaining ground in her communication with Margie?

Every time she had thought she had reached a new level, she slipped backward again. The day when she had almost missed the grade-level meeting and had not prepared for the after-school program discussion was just one example. What about Amberlee? Was she applying the four pillars with her? If she was completely honest with herself, the news that Amberlee was transferring to Jackson had shaken her a little. The challenge to practice what she preached was not one that Sarah took lightly. She would embrace this adventure like anything else she had done in her life, with full enthusiasm and taking the full force of it, the good and the bad, with her mind and heart wide open.

The lively conversation in the teacher's lounge had been just the first of a long-term trend. Every day one of the teachers seemed to bring up one or more of the four pillars in casual conversation. Either by retelling something that had happened in their homes with their families or in the classroom with the students, *Quality Conversations* was now a staple topic of discussion. What struck Sarah the most was how completely natural it seemed for them to be talking about it. Sarah was marveling at this on the last day of work before the Christmas break. They were gathered in the teacher's lounge exchanging good wishes and complaining, as was the custom, about how hurried it all felt during the season.

"I've been rushed off my feet with shopping and decorations," Amy told Sarah as a group of teachers gathered for their coffee break.

"What are you doing for the holidays Sarah?" Ed asked.

"I'm spending it at the farm, with my parents and my sister and her husband," she said.

"That's nice," Amy said, "then all you have to do is shop for presents and show up. That's the beauty of the single life; nobody expects you to be the host."

"Well, I do help out with some of the preparations," Sarah said, laughing, "but I guess you're right. Mostly I just show up and enjoy!"

"Are you traveling to Seattle, Ed?" Amy asked.

"Yes," he said, "although I don't look forward to crowded airports and potential weather delays."

"Big family gathering?" another teacher asked Ed.

"Huge," Ed replied, "we are six brothers, all married with children." He paused and grimaced. "Except for me, I suppose, I'm not married any longer. That will be weird; the first Christmas as a born-again bachelor."

"I don't get it at all," another teacher said, "all these preparations and expense only to end up fighting like mad dogs over the smallest thing. Everybody goes back home cranky, tired, and nursing indigestion. Ho-ho-ho!"

"That's true for most families, unfortunately," Amy agreed, "I already know to sit my father-in-law as far away as I can from my uncle, but no matter how perfectly I plan it they always seem to find each other and it's a full twelve-round heavyweight verbal match. They always find something to disagree about; if it's not the local election it could be the color of the tablecloth. It makes it so unpleasant for everyone."

"I know," Sarah said, "just a few weeks ago at Thanksgiving there was this huge blowup at the dinner table. Guess who started it? Me! And I didn't intend to do it! Far from it! I don't like confrontation, let alone arguments at family holidays."

"The thing is," says Ed, "that sometimes these arguments have a life of their own. We all put our best foot forward but I suppose that we all get to the holidays so tired and overstretched, that it takes the smallest provocation to ignite a bonfire…it's a miracle we don't end up on the ten o'clock news."

"You know what?" Amy said, "it occurs to me that the holidays are a perfect time to put the four pillars into practice."

They all nodded and looked at Sarah.

"Here we go," Sarah smiled, "I'm in the spotlight again."

"There's no getting away from it now, kid," said Amy.

"I think that's brilliant," said Ed, "like an experiment. How about it Sarah?"

"Sounds more like an assignment," Sarah said, "people are going to end up hating the sight of me."

"On the contrary," Ed said, "I think it will be fun. How about if we all go to our respective gatherings and parties and share the four pillars with our families and try to put them into practice and see what happens?"

"Perfect," said another teacher, "then when we come back we can all compare notes."

"I like it," Amy said, "this will take my mind off having to keep my relatives from scratching each other's eyeballs."

"It would be really good research for your after-school program," Ed said to Sarah, arching his eyebrows as if expecting her reply.

104

"But it's the last day," Sarah hesitated, "it would be hard to pass the word around."

"I'll ask everyone in my grade, and I'll talk to Mr. Coles," Amy said, "Ed, you could do the same for your grade."

There was a pause as they all waited for Sarah's reaction.

"Let's do it!" she said.

By the end of the day, as they all left for the holidays, word had spread through the school. The teachers passing her in the corridor and even in the parking lot gave Sarah a knowing nod, as if a secret society had just been formed, charged with new purpose as they all scattered in their separate ways to join their loved ones and celebrate the season.

Transformation

There was a marked difference in Sarah as she made the trip home for Christmas. On the early morning flight to Dallas she read over her notes and the passages she had marked in the book and put them into the order they would appear in the after-school program, and the long drive was made short by setting her Dictaphone to record and leaving it on the passenger seat. By thinking out loud as if she was explaining the four pillars to an audience, and adding ideas and reminders to use in setting the structure for the after-school program, by the time she approached her parents home in Winnsboro she had collected a good amount of raw material for her work. As soon as she pulled into the driveway, the front door opened and the familiar silhouette of her father lingered for a moment. He walked to her car and opened the door for her. Sarah jumped out and put her arms around his waist, holding on a few moments longer than usual.

"It's so good to see you, Dad," she said. "I missed you."

"I missed you too kid," he said, softly, and then in a more upbeat tone, "there's no one sensible to talk to around here when you're gone," he joked, "well, apart from Noah, but he's working most of the time. He likes to work, go figure."

They went inside where Sarah's mother and her sister were baking cupcakes for the church bazaar and Sarah quickly unpacked her things in her old bedroom to join them in the kitchen. It was an odd feeling to be a guest in your own home, a mixture of detachment and belonging. A Chinese proverb came to her mind: You cannot swim in the same river twice. The room was the same but it was the person who had changed, a change that could be measured not just in length of years but in events and feelings, internal benchmarks that were as real as the notches on the doorframe marking her height over the years. At five foot five the growth had stopped, and it was coincidentally at the same time the internal changes had really taken over. Sarah looked at the pictures on the wall, framed posters of poetry and horses, and recognized that the little girl that chose those pictures was still very much alive inside her. She wondered if it was the same with everyone else, that feeling of duality, of being an adult and a child at the same time. She thought about the conversation with her colleagues in the teacher's room, about the arguments that overtake family gatherings.

Sarah began to realize that there is a recognizable pattern in conversations that go awry; one person turns into an overbearing parent, and another acts up like a fussy child. It is only when both parties come back to the adult-to-adult level that any proper communication can be achieved. She was thinking mostly of pillar number three. There is absolutely no point in giving feedback to someone who is acting like a child, or in receiving feedback from someone who is acting as a judgmental authoritarian. The only way for feedback to be effective is for it to be exchanged among adults. Not an adult in the strict sense of the age of the communicator, but rather in the role and attitude that the person is taking in the conversation. She added a comment in her notepad to include this thought in the program.

Sarah joined her mother and sister in the kitchen and lost herself in the delight of decorating the cupcakes. Using colored icing and glitter sugar, she created a selection of holiday motifs from Santa's hats to Christmas trees and sprigs of holly. The ample kitchen table overflowed with red, green, and white sparkling confections giving off such a festive effect that even Noah, normally oblivious to the finer workings of the baking arts, was lending a hand packing them for transport.

"They look really pretty," said Gayle, admiring the work.

"They do," said their mother.

"I think we should try one before we take them over," said Sarah's dad, hovering over the table, "don't you agree Noah? Quality control?"

Sarah's mother playfully shooed him away so he perched on the window seat and munched on an apple instead.

"So how's the job going kiddo?" he asked.

"Pretty good, actually," Sarah said, as she piped icing on another cupcake, "this extraordinary thing happened. Suddenly I am now in charge of an after-school program."

"Really?" Noah said, "that sounds like a big responsibility."

"Specially for your first year," Gayle said, "is that normal?"

109

"When has Sarah ever done anything within the norm?" said her mother, without looking up from her cupcakes but smiling with pride.

"Well, it's not official yet," Sarah said, "the principal still has to approve it. But it's going pretty well."

"So what is it about?" asked her Dad.

"Well, it actually started after a conversation with Noah," Sarah said, "and a paper that our principal gave me to read."

Noah blushed and put even more concentration to arranging the cupcakes in the plastic food containers.

"Don't be humble, Noah," Sarah said, looking at Gayle, "he deserves the credit."

Sarah related how the conversation with Noah had given her insight into how Mr. Cole's paper on quality conversations related to practical real-life situations. She then went on to explain the assignment that all the teachers had undertaken over the holidays, to try the four pillars of *Quality Conversations* at home with their friends and families over the holidays.

"That sounds like a good idea," said Gayle, "if they survive the Christmas excesses, that means that they are solid as can be."

"We should try them here," said her Dad, "then you would have more examples for your program."

"Really?" Sarah asked, "you wouldn't mind?"

"Of course," her mother said, "but you'll have to remind me about what those four things were when we get back from the bazaar because right now my mind is in two places. It's almost time to go."

110

They all managed to get into Sarah's rental car, except for Noah, who slowly drove along in the pick-up truck with the delicate cupcake cargo. The church bazaar was a tradition that Sarah had never failed to attend every since she could remember.

"Isn't it great that Noah is coming with us this year?" Sarah said to Gayle and to her parents in the car, watching Noah drive ahead of them.

"He's a good man," her mother said, "we are lucky to have him in the family."

"You were afraid that the family would get smaller when we grew up, Mom," Sarah said, "but it's the opposite. We're getting bigger! Now we are arriving in two cars instead of one!"

Sarah looked at Gayle in the rear-view mirror and noticed she had a knowing smile, as if she had something to say but was waiting for the right moment. When they arrived at the church Sarah took her sister to one side.

"I know that face. You look like the cat that swallowed the canary," Sarah said, "what's up?"

Gayle whispered into Sarah's ear the words that she most wanted to hear.

"You are going to be an auntie…" Gayle murmured, and quickly put her finger to Sarah's lips, "but don't say a word until I tell Mom and Dad! I want to tell them on Christmas, like a gift except it doesn't need wrapping."

Sarah agreed. It was the best gift in the world.

The church hall was buzzing with activity, children playing, women exchanging greetings, men gathering in one corner talking about sports. On the opposite end near the wide doors Sarah spotted a familiar face that she hadn't seen in a long time. It was her fourth grade teacher, Mrs. Lee, a tiny gentle figure that had retained her good posture and kind eyes. She had aged gracefully. Sarah made her way over.

"Hello Mrs. Lee. It's Sarah. Do you remember me?"

Mrs. Lee looked up at Sarah's face. A moment passed before the glint of recognition wrinkled the corners of Mrs. Lee's face.

"Sarah Granger!" she said, "how nice to see you. Of course I remember. How have you been?"

"Really good," Sarah said, "I'm a teacher now."

"Wonderful," Mrs. Lee said, "best job in the world."

It was amazing that Mrs. Lee still loved teaching after all these years. Surely she must have had her own share of obstacles and challenges, but somehow she had never lost her passion for it.

"I hear you're retired now," Sarah said.

"Yes, and I miss it every day," said Mrs. Lee, "but I still occasionally help out at different schools in the district, just to keep nimble."

"They are lucky to have you," Sarah said, "What do you help with?"

"The after-school programs," said Mrs. Lee, beaming her smile, "whenever they have to set up a new one or revitalize one that is going a bit slow, they call me. I love it."

"I would love to talk to you about that," Sarah said.

"Sure, let's find a quiet corner," said Mrs. Lee, and she led the way towards the stage area with a sprightly step.

GALE A. LEE & ALICE M. SPENCE

She pushed two chairs closer together on one side of the stage exit, slightly sheltered from the crowded room by a brightly lit Christmas tree. Sarah bought them two cups of hot cocoa and two of the homemade cupcakes and set them down on the edge of the stage. In their snug little corner, Sarah related to her teacher her difficulties at the beginning of the school year and how her interest in *Quality Conversations* had developed into the assignment of setting up a new after-school program. Mrs. Lee followed intently, biting with relish into the cupcake.

"This is delicious," she said.

"My Mom made them," Sara said, proudly, "I decorated them."

Mrs. Lee patted Sarah's wrist affectionately, as if congratulating her for all her entire achievements in one simple gesture. She then mulled over what Sarah had said for a few moments.

"Tell me more about the four pillars," she said.

"The four pillars are: Listening, Asking Questions, Giving and Receiving Feedback and Reflection," Sarah explained.

She then expanded a little on the meaning of each and gave a few examples of her own experience of the four pillars at work and in her personal life.

"Very interesting," Mrs. Lee nodded, "I think this after-school program could do a lot of good. I think you have received some precious knowledge, Sarah, and now you are in charge of passing it on to others."

"You don't think it's too soon?" Sarah said, "To be in charge of a program in my first year at work? I thought I

113

would need more experience, more maturity before taking on something of that scope."

Mrs. Lee smiled with her eyes closed, as if she knew an ancient secret that she was about to reveal.

"Yours is no ordinary talent, Sarah," Mrs. Lee said, leaning forward, "I remember you very well from my class. You have an open mind, an inquisitive nature. It would be unreasonable to expect that your career would unfold in the traditional way."

"I'm trying to accept it, but my heart skips a beat when I think about being in charge of this," Sarah said, "I admit that I sometimes feel I am not competent to do it. Jackson is one of the most prestigious schools around; it's traditional and innovative at the same time. Things are done a certain way. People are used to certain systems. Here I am a newcomer, fresh from college, trying to tell them how they should change their communication habits and embrace a new way of talking to each other!"

"As you know, some of us learn better by listening, some of us learn better by reading," said Mrs. Lee, "but all of us learn better by doing. Don't *tell* them what to do, *show* them how to do it. It is only natural that you'll face resistance to change in the beginning, and you should expect some of them to be downright obstructive, even people who you think are the best candidates for it, the ones who need it the most. I tell you what, you can call me or email me anytime, day or night. As I get older, I don't need much sleep anyway," she said, winking.

"That's is so generous of you," Sarah said, "I'll take you up on the offer. I just hope I am not giving rise to unreasonable expectations."

"Remember the words of George Bernard Shaw," said Mrs. Lee.

"What's that?" asked Sarah.

"The reasonable man adapts himself to the world; the unreasonable one persists in trying to adapt the world to himself. Therefore all progress depends on the unreasonable man."

Christmas day arrived with a cold snap. Sarah could see her breath in the early morning air as she shuffled to her car to get the presents. She trotted back and arranged them under the tree, just as her mother was coming out of the kitchen with a steaming mug of coffee.

"I hope the others get over here soon," her mother said, "I can't wait to open my presents!"

Christmas morning made everybody feel a little like a child again. Her mother, more than anyone else, turned into a bright-eyed girl at the sight of a Christmas trees loaded with brightly wrapped packages. A couple of hours later Gayle and Noah arrived and Sarah's father came back in from the barn.

"OK, we're all here," said Sarah's mother, "let's start!"

"Wait," her husband said, "I'll get some eggnog."

"It's too early for that!" she said.

"It's Christmas," he said, "time for a little indulgence."

"You better go easy on your stomach," she said, "I do not want to spend Christmas in the hospital."

"Don't be dramatic, woman," he said, grunting—but conceded and sat down on the sofa.

115

Neither of the two is listening to the other, Sarah thought.

"Folks," Sarah said, "time to do your homework. You are not listening to each other. Pillar number one. Listening."

"That's right," her Dad chimed in, "pillar one. Tell your mother."

At that moment, Gayle stood up in front of the Christmas tree.

"Before we do the presents," Gayle said, "I'd like to give you the first gift of the day. Mom, Dad…. you're going to be grandparents!"

Both parents jumped up and hugged Gayle, and Sarah and Noah joined them.

"That's it!" said their father, "I'm getting that eggnog!"

This time his wife did not object. "Get some for me too!" she said.

❧

Back at home, Sarah had time to reflect. This had been one of the happiest holidays she could remember, and next year promised to be even better, with a new baby in the family. The Quality Conversations experiment had gone well. There had been no arguments, conversations had flowed easily, and everyone seemed to be at ease. But was it because everyone involved knew they were part of the test or was it genuinely the four pillars at work? It was hard to tell.

She kept that factor in mind as she filtered through the feedback that her colleagues had gleaned upon their return from their respective family gatherings. It was the first day back at work after the break and both the teachers

116

and students were slightly distracted. Sarah made a conscious effort to refrain her enthusiasm about the findings that the other teachers had handed over to her. The general feedback had been positive; they all had found that one or more of the pillars had worked for them. There was one notable exception; it was a simple note from Ed. It just said: "Sorry, unable to gather feedback for the QC program. Nothing wrong with the four pillars, just not the right time to test them." Another slight setback came in the form of Amberlee. It was her first day at Jackson. She took Sarah aside in the teacher's lounge.

"Why didn't you tell me about this assignment you gave out to everyone?" she asked Sarah in a clipped tone.

"It's not an assignment," Sarah said, "It wasn't even my idea. It came up spontaneously, on the last day before the break."

"I feel left out," Amberlee said, "everyone's talking about it."

"I'm sorry," Sarah said, although she was not sure what she was apologizing for, "it never occurred to me, as you hadn't started yet. Besides, it was voluntary, nobody *had* to do it."

"Well," Amberlee said, "you know I've got your back. I just thought you'd have mine."

"But I do," Sarah said.

Later that evening, at home, she wondered whether Amberlee's presence at Jackson would just make things more complicated. She tried to shake the thought and put Amberlee's reaction down to anxiety over the new job and overexcitement of the holidays. Deciding to pour all her effort into the after-school program, she worked on the final details for her presentation to Mr. Cole and made it an early night.

❦

The meeting with Mr. Coles was set just before lunch while her students were in their music lesson so Sarah knew that she should keep it short and to the point. Mr. Coles listened to her presentation with full attention, never interrupting, until Sarah had taken him through the proposed structure for the program. She had used all her research and the pointers that Mrs. Lee had given her, as well as the feedback from the other teachers and material from the book. The result was a well thought out, fluid program that provided a balanced mix of planned activities and time for open discussion.

"I like it," Mr. Coles said, "leave it with me, I'd like to discuss it with a couple of other people and get back to you. I'll let you know tomorrow."

Sarah was surprised. She had anticipated that the decision would take weeks.

"That's soon! Well, thank you," Sarah said, and got up to leave, "and let me know if you have any questions."

"I will," said Mr. Coles, "Oh, and Sarah, if it gets approved, be ready to start in as soon as two weeks. Do you think you could handle it?"

Sarah's head was reeling. Two weeks! She thought of her conversation with Mrs. Lee.

"Sure," Sarah said, smiling, "two weeks sounds great."

She walked back to her classroom to grab her lunch bag. *Two weeks sounds great? I can't believe I just said that. Mrs. Lee had better meant her offer of help, because I'm going to need it.*

It was a beautiful blue-sky day, and Sarah took her lunch bag out and sat under a tree. Soon she heard footsteps.

"Mind if I join you?" Ed said.

"Sure," she replied.

"It's such a beautiful day, isn't it?" Ed said, as he settled on a sunny spot on the other side of the tree.

"A picnic in the middle of winter," Sarah smiled, "bet you can't do that in Seattle."

Sarah didn't want to pry so she decided she would not bring up the note about the QC feedback if Ed didn't mention it. She was sure that he would bring it up if he felt like talking about it, and, sure enough, he did.

"I wanted to explain about the QC assignment," Ed said.

"You don't need to explain, Ed," Sarah said, "don't worry about it. I got plenty of feedback as it is, and you helped get everybody involved, so you did more than help already."

"I don't mind telling you," Ed said, "I just didn't want to say it in front of the others, to avoid questions."

"Ah, Pillar number two," Sarah said.

"Exactly," Ed laughed softly, "the thing is that I was supposed to meet my ex-wife in Seattle. Our two families are used to celebrating together, and we discussed it, and she thought it was a good idea to keep the tradition. So she suggested that we get together as usual and use the opportunity to see if there was any chance of us..."

119

Ed paused, took a sip of his soda, and continued.

"Of us getting back together. It was her idea, you know," he said, "she called me. Anyway. I flew to Seattle, as you know, and we all got together Christmas Eve at her parents' as usual. Then we were going to spend Christmas Day at my folks, again the two families together, a big group of people. My family is huge. So I thought, what could be a better opportunity to test the four pillars of *Quality Conversations*, right?"

"Sounds like it," Sarah said, then waited for a moment before asking, "so what happened?"

"She didn't show up," he said, and swallowed hard.

Sarah didn't say anything. On the one hand she was giving Ed time to recover, but on the other hand, she didn't know what to say. How can anybody do that? To give hope and then to withdraw it seemed indefensible and cruel.

"She's not evil," Ed said after a few moments, "I think in truth she is weak. She runs away from things. Doesn't confront them."

"Did she say why she didn't show up?" Sarah asked.

"She didn't have to," he said, "I received a strange text from her on my mobile, giving a flight and time of arrival, but it was to the wrong airport, in another city. It took me a while to realize that she had meant to send the text to the other guy, the one she was really meeting for Christmas."

"Oh, Ed," Sarah said, "how awful!"

"Pretty horrible," Ed said, trying to smile but failing, "goes to show, better check twice that you're sending the text to the right person! I replied to her text and that's

120

when she realized that she had sent it to me instead of him. I felt bad for her family, as well, having to go through the motions of a happy holiday party. They were really embarrassed; it took them by surprise."

"Did you tell them about the text message?" Sarah said.

"No," he said, "I just said that she couldn't make it. No point in rubbing it in. It wasn't their fault. I should have known. It's not the first time. You expect someone to change, you expect them to get it, but it is just your wishful thinking. Nobody changes. Keep that in mind when you get married, Sarah. Pick someone who you like just as he is, because he's not going to change."

"I suppose so," Sarah said, "and the lying makes it worse…if you can't have an honest conversation with the person you are married to, then there is not much hope to achieve any significant communication, is there?"

"Precisely," Ed said, "so now you know why I didn't contribute to your feedback. There wasn't much point in testing the four pillars in a room full of lies and half-truths."

"I'm so sorry you had to go through that," Sarah said, "but you just made a very good point. The whole principle of a quality conversation has to rest on the basis of the integrity of the communication. There can't be any insincerity or any intention to deceive on either part. People have to say what they mean and mean what they say."

"Maybe it is worth pointing that out at the beginning of your program," Ed said, "you can't have a quality conversation if only one of the parties is invested in the process; everybody needs to participate fully. I guess that works for the third pillar as well, giving and receiving feedback."

121

"Exactly," Sarah, "the feedback has to have the same integrity as the rest of the conversation, otherwise it is worthless. When you give and receive feedback, it is important to keep it meaningful. See what I mean? You've already contributed a very important point."

"That makes me feel useful," Ed said, crumpling the wrapper of his sandwich and stuffing it into his empty paper bag, "anyway, water under the bridge, new year, new life. So how's the after-school QC program coming along?"

"I met with Mr. Coles today," Sarah said, "and if it goes ahead it will happen quickly so I'll need all your help."

"You got it," Ed said, helping Sarah to get up, "so how was your Christmas? Everybody showed up? No text messages?"

They both laughed and on their way back inside Sarah told Ed about the baby news, and about the meeting with her teacher Mrs. Lee. As they parted, Ed turned to Sarah.

"I'm glad we talked, Sarah," Ed said, "I didn't want to drop this load on you, but I also didn't want you to think that I had forgotten about the feedback. You know how it is, away from family, new city, new friends. When you go through a rough patch it can feel lonely. Thanks for listening."

"Hey," Sarah said, "no problem. One day it will be me unloading on you so you'll have plenty of chances to return the favor."

The following afternoon after school was over, Mr. Coles caught up with Sarah in the parking lot as she was getting in to her car to drive home.

"Sarah," Mr. Coles waved, "wait up."

He was slightly out of breath as he approached her car window as Sarah was rolling it down.

"Green light on the QC program," he said, "we start two weeks from Thursday."

"Holy cow!" Sarah whooped, then caught herself, and cupped her hand on her mouth, "I'm sorry! It just came out!"

They both laughed, and Sarah drove off bursting with pride and excitement about having her own after-school program approved on the first attempt. She would leave the nerves and doubts for later; right now it was time to enjoy and relish the anticipation.

That evening was the standing dinner meeting with Amberlee at the pizza place. Sarah couldn't wait to share with Amberlee the news about her program. This time she would make sure to involve her right from the start so she wouldn't feel left out. Sarah was led to her table. She chose the chair facing the entrance, but instead of Amberlee, she found herself staring at Tom, the object of Amberlee's daydreams. He recognized her immediately. He approached her and leaned over in a half-hug, half-air kiss that Sarah found friendly and endearing.

"Hi Tom," she said.

"Sarah, " he said and slid into the chair opposite her, "it's so nice to see you."

"I heard this is your favorite restaurant," Sarah said.

"Get the pasta e faggioli," he said, "worth every calorie. I'm meeting two of my clients with their wives. Are you expecting someone?"

123

"Our mutual friend actually," Sarah said, "I'm having dinner with Amberlee."

"Pity," he said, "otherwise you could have joined us, so I wouldn't be the third wheel, or the fifth wheel rather. Maybe next time I should give you advance notice."

Sarah smiled. Was this his roundabout way of asking her for her number? In any case, he already had her email address from the book club, so it would be easy for him to reach her if he felt like it. Tom had such warmth about him, Sarah felt as if he had known him for a long time.

"So you are hosting the next book club, right?" Tom said.

"Yes, I am," Sarah said.

"I'm looking forward to seeing you in your home turf," he said.

"Don't expect too much," Sarah said, "we'll be lucky if we can squeeze everyone in."

"It'll be fine," he said, "I can come by early if you need any help setting up? I can bring some food, too. I make a mean guacamole."

"I know. Amberlee said you're quite the gourmet," Sarah said, "but she said she's going to help me, so thanks but I think I'm fine."

"So you two have been talking about me then," Tom said, smiling from the corner of his mouth.

"It came up in conversation," Sarah said, smiling back.

At that moment, she noticed Amberlee standing outside the entrance, looking at them. Why wasn't she coming in? Sarah waved her over.

"There she is," Sarah said.

124

"Oops," he said, turning around and waving at someone, "there's my client. I better join them."

Just like that that Tom disappeared deeper into the restaurant and Amberlee took his place. Sarah felt her cheeks blush as she realized what this might have looked like from Amberlee's point of view. Further, she realized that Tom might have misinterpreted, thinking that the interest in him had come from Sarah, instead of Amberlee. So much for the quality of this conversation!

"Was that Tom?" Amberlee asked, her eyes darting around the room.

"You know it was," Sarah said, "and it's not what it looked like. He's here with some clients and he spotted me waiting for you."

"Did he know I was coming?" she asked.

"Yes, but his clients just arrived and he couldn't wait," Sarah said, feeling as if she was making excuses for Tom.

"So what did you two talk about?" Amberlee asked.

"He said to get the pasta e faggioli," Sarah replied.

"Well, let's do that then," Amberlee said as the server approached.

After they ordered, Sarah changed of subject.

"So how are you settling in at Jackson, do you like it?"

"Great," Amberlee said, smiling now, "everyone is so nice. I couldn't possibly ask for a better school."

"We are lucky," Sarah said.

"And Mr. Coles," Amberlee continued, "he's so nice. He even came up to me at church on Sunday and said he was looking forward to having me on his team."

"He's a gentleman," Sarah said.

125

"So how's your thing going?" Amberlee asked.

"The QC program?" Sarah said, "I just heard that it was approved so we're starting in two weeks. I'll need all your help."

"Wow," she said, her eyes widening, "two weeks. That soon?"

"Terrifying, I know," Sarah said, "but it's on an experimental basis. If it doesn't click, they'll just replace it with the next idea."

"And if it works?" Amberlee asked.

"Then it could get rolled out to other schools in the district."

"It could get big," Amberlee said.

"I'd rather not think about that now," Sarah said, "it's too scary. I'll just concentrate on getting it going."

"Baby steps," Amberlee nodded, "sounds smart. I'm afraid I don't have any experience to help you with this."

"Neither have I," Sarah said, "my fourth grade teacher, Mrs. Lee, who is now retired, has become a consultant in this field, and she offered to help."

"Maybe it would be better if I remain as an outsider," Amberlee said, "that way I can give you really objective feedback. If I am too involved it would taint my point of view."

"I guess," Sarah said, unconvinced, "it's just that I thought you wanted to be a part of it."

"Of course," Amberlee said, "and as your critical peer, I would be observing and picking up comments from participants and being your eyes and ears, but with a healthy professional distance."

126

The conversation then flowed from the talk about work to the preparations for the upcoming book club meeting.

"Don't worry about the book club people," Amberlee said, "they are really great, and I'll help you get ready."

Sarah took a sharp breath.

"What?" Amberlee asked.

"The book club meeting," Sarah said, "it's two weeks from Thursday, and the same day the QC program starts."

"You're right," Amberlee said.

"I can't possibly do both," Sarah said, "Can we reschedule the book club?"

"I don't know," Amberlee said, "What time is the QC program?"

"The first day it's just an open familiarization session for people to sign up, from five thirty to six p.m," Sarah said, "and the book club meeting is at seven."

"We can push the book club to seven thirty p.m., and I'll go to your apartment and prepare everything. You won't have to move a finger; just show up. Even if you are a little late we can start without you. It will be fun, it can help you relax, and the following day you can sleep in. Isn't the field trip to the dairy farm that Friday?"

"Yes, you're right," Sarah said, still not convinced.

"There you go," Amberlee said, "just tell Margie you'll be coming later Friday. She won't mind as the kids won't be there."

Sarah would have preferred to cancel the book club evening altogether at this time when she was concentrating her energy on the QC program, but as Amberlee was so intent on keeping it going, she decided to allow

127

it to happen. If Amberlee organized everything as she said there would be very little for her to do. Besides, in all probability, Amberlee was looking forward to seeing Tom and if there was anything Sarah could do to make this happen, then it would just be awkward not to do it.

Sarah suspected, however, that the interest was mostly on Amberlee's side. She hadn't sensed any particular spark from Tom; otherwise it would have been natural for him to linger for a few moments at the table when Amberlee arrived. It was not up to Sarah, in any case, to find this out; it would all work out as it would. When it came to matters of the heart, she thought, the signals can get mixed and the messages can be easily missed. This was one area where she would steer clear of trying to apply the four pillars, at least until she became a black belt at *Quality Conversations* herself.

The day finally arrived. Today was the open session of the Quality Conversations after-school program. The purpose of this first encounter was to present the program and give the opportunity to teachers, parents, and students to ask questions and sign up for the QC program that would take place every Thursday after that. They were unsure of how many people would attend, so Mr. Coles had asked Sarah to hold the session in the auditorium. He would assign a permanent room to the program once they knew how many participants actually signed up, if any.

Sarah would have preferred to hold the session in a more intimate setting, but she could see the point of having this space, just in case. She was busy testing the projector for her slide presentation, when Margie arrived, carrying the sign-up forms. They had a short description of the program, what would be expected of the participants, the schedule, and the information to sign up in person, by phone, or email.

"Good luck, Sarah," Margie said, "Do you want these up front or in the back?"

"Where would you recommend?" Sarah asked.

"I would leave a stack up front for you, and then we could hand them out in the back as they leave, so we make sure everybody has a copy."

"That sounds good," Sarah said. "Thanks, Margie. I'm a little nervous, so I appreciate the support."

Margie broke into a wide smile. "No problem. I'll assign a couple of students to each door to hand them out."

Margie took a seat at the very back of the auditorium. To see a person actually sitting there in the audience made it all become real for Sarah. She felt as if a shock of electricity had rushed up from her stomach to her throat. One by one the seats started to fill up as scattered groups of parents and their children arrived. Soon the auditorium was humming with people, alive with the sounds of voices, candy wrappers, and children's chatter. Sarah was slightly surprised by the number of people, but she reasoned that many of them might just be here accompanying others, rather than interested in the program in particular. Finally the teachers, staff, and Mr. Coles took their seats in the front rows that Sarah had reserved for them. It was time.

129

"Welcome everyone, parents, students, staff, and visitors," Sarah addressed the crowd through the microphone, "my name is Sarah Granger, and I will be your host for the *Quality Conversations* after-school program. The aim of this program is to provide the tools to get better at communicating with each other. What we will learn here applies to the classroom, the office, the home, even the playground. Let me tell you a little about how the idea for this program came about."

Sarah walked the audience briefly through the four pillars and how Mr. Coles had sparked her interest in them with the paper, then the books she had read, and the feedback that the teachers had collected over the holidays.

"Everyone seems to agree that there is something of value here," Sarah said, "and we would like to share it with you so that what our students learn in the classroom and what your children live at home can reinforce and support each other. We believe that not only students but also parents and teachers can all benefit from this program. This is not the type of learning that is dictated from the front of the room, rather it is through the participation of each one of you that we all become richer."

Sarah opened the floor for questions. After a few technical questions about materials or minimal attendance required, Sarah declared the session over.

"Please pick up a sign-in form before you leave," Sarah said, "and if any of you would like to sign up right now, please come to the front and leave your forms with me."

To Sarah's surprised, Margie's voice boomed from the back of the room.

"Don't worry, Sarah," Margie shouted, "nobody gets past me without taking home a leaflet!"

The room erupted with laughter as Margie was handed the microphone. With her impeccable appearance and commanding poise, she addressed the room with the authority that comes from experience.

"I urge all of you to attend the QC program," Margie said, "it is one of the best we have ever had, and Ms. Granger has done a superb job of making it both interesting and fun. I have had the opportunity to test these pillars myself, and I tell you, they work. Don't let this opportunity go by. It is like getting the best recipe for brownies, you'll end up using it over and over."

As laughter rippled across the audience Sarah was delighted with Margie's support and glad that she had the opportunity to see an entirely different side to her. She remembered Mr. Cole's words: "Margie has such experience and balance—she'll be a great resource for you." Although Sarah had failed to see these qualities when she had just met Margie, she was glad that she could now understand what he meant. Once again, the application of the four pillars in her meetings with Margie had allowed them to reach this point of mutual respect, the point that marked the balance of quality communications. If it hadn't been for the four pillars who knows what her relationship with her grade-level chair would be like now, and who knows if she would still be working at Jackson? It could all have gone very wrong, but instead something was going very, very right.

On any regular day the drive back home from school took Sarah between twenty and twenty-five minutes, but this evening the roads were surprisingly clear. The traffic lights seemed to be aligned in her favor and so she reached home just in time to greet the guests coming to the book club meeting. As she inserted the key in the lock of her one-bedroom apartment, the door opened and Amberlee greeted her with oven mitts on her hands.

"That was quick!" Amberlee said, "How did it go?"

"Pretty smooth. Margie was great," Sarah said, "we'll see how many people sign up."

Sarah slung her bag and jacket on the coat rack by the entrance door. Amberlee had pushed the small dining table against the wall to make more space and had placed tea lights all along the counter that separated the cooking area from the rest of the room. The four folding dining chairs were arranged around the sitting area and the low coffee table was brimming with bowls of pita bread cut into small triangles, hummus and tsatsiki, plates of vine-leaf wraps, and plum tomatoes stuffed with mozzarella and basil.

"I went Mediterranean," Amberlee said, holding her mittened hands up like a surgeon, "there's chicken kebabs grilling in the oven and baklava for dessert."

"It looks great," Sarah said, "I'm starving."

Just then Tom emerged from the bathroom.

"Oh, hello Tom, I didn't realize you were here," Sarah said.

GALE A. LEE & ALICE M. SPENCE

"Hi Sarah," Tom greeted her, with his familiar one-arm hug, "I just put out some extra guest towels in the bathroom. Was everything OK with your event?"

"Yes, thank you," she said, "can I give you a hand here?"

"Absolutely not," Amberlee said, handing her a glass of white wine, "just sit down and relax."

As Amberlee busied herself with the oven, Tom sat beside Sarah on the couch.

"Amberlee asked me if I could come earlier to help you," Tom said softly, "I didn't know you wouldn't be here. Am I right to think you didn't know about it?"

Sarah picked up a slight edge in Tom's voice.

"I didn't know," she said, "but I still appreciate the help."

"It's not that I mind helping," Tom said, "the thing is that…"

Tom stopped mid-sentence as the doorbell rang. Sarah got up and greeted the first group of people. Soon the rest arrived. All sixteen of them managed to fit comfortably in her small lounge, perched on armrests and sitting on cushions on the floor. The food was delicious and soon the conversation was flowing easily.

"That was an absolute joy," Sarah said to Amberlee as the last of the guests had left, "thanks so much for all your help."

"You're welcome," Amberlee said, "I told you it would be all right, didn't I?"

"You were right," Sarah said, "Listen, Amberlee, do you mind if I ask you about something. It's not really a pleasant thing but…"

133

"You must be exhausted," Amberlee cut her off, "and frankly, I'm a little tired myself. Can we talk about it tomorrow?"

Sarah reluctantly agreed and said goodbye to Amberlee. She had intended to ask about Tom and what Sarah hoped was a misunderstanding with the request for help on her behalf. Unfortunately, Sarah suspected that there was no such misunderstanding and that Amberlee had arranged it so that she would have Tom to herself, which Sarah didn't mind, as long as she hadn't misled Tom to think that it was Sarah who had engineered it. She made herself a cup of herbal tea before going to bed and checked her email. There was a message from Tom. He just wrote his mobile number and asked Sarah to please call him so they could finish their interrupted conversation. It was obvious that the situation hadn't sat well with Tom either. It had been a big day and it was probably too late to call that evening, so Sarah entered Tom's number in the memory of her mobile to call him the following day.

Mr. Coles stopped by Sarah's classroom the next morning to congratulate her on the presentation. She was alone, catching up on paperwork since her class had gone out on the farm field trip.

"Do you know how many people signed up for QC?" Mr. Coles asked.

"Not yet. The email registrations are coming in so I guess we should have a good idea by Monday."

134

"I'm very proud of you, Sarah," Mr. Coles said, "I know it was a tight schedule but you came through for Jackson."

"Thank you, Mr. Coles," Sarah said, "it was terrifying and exhilarating at the same time."

"You have initiative, Sarah," he said, "and that's something that can't be taught. It is in your temperament. I've noticed an improvement in our communications among teachers and staff ever since we started talking about QC. I can see it in our meetings."

"That's great," Sarah said, "but the credit goes to you for creating the space for this to happen. I just added a little manpower to the existing effort."

"You added more than that," he said, "but it is too easy for an initiative like this to lose steam and get buried in the humdrum of routine. I don't want this to happen. So I've been thinking that if the program goes well, once you've settled into it, I'd like you to consider another task."

Sarah leaned forward.

"I know you have a full plate with all this," Mr. Coles said, "but I'd like you to be a part of the staff development team."

Sarah knew how unusual it was for a new teacher to be invited to such a key team within such a prestigious school, so she knew better than question Mr. Cole's judgment in offering it to her.

"Thanks!" Sarah said, "I'm really flattered."

"I want to make *Quality Conversations* part of our everyday communication strategy until it becomes second nature," Mr. Coles said, "Unfortunately, not everyone in the staff is on board. Once your QC program is

135

under way you will probably find that I am right. Quite a few of the people that are all smiles and cheers right now are simply going through the motions but not really taking the four pillars to heart. There will be open resistance, which you are trained to handle. That is just one battle but it doesn't win the war. The most difficult attitude, however, much worse than resistance, is indifference. That is the real challenge. Indifference is the silent killer of meaningful progress."

Mr. Coles left Sarah to mull over his words. She was excited about the offer to join the development team and concerned about her ability to handle what Mr. Coles had identified as the biggest challenge. She would have to pay attention to the silent indifference. The voice of resistance was easy to identify, but there was the risk to have the squeaky wheel get all the attention and not work enough on the indifferent participants that fall by the wayside. She would have to be on the alert. She had been warned.

A few minutes after Mr. Coles left, as Sarah was delving back into her work, she heard voices in the corridor. At first she thought it was one voice, rather loud, but soon it was evident that it was more than one person involved and they were arguing. Sarah got up from her desk and peeked outside. It sounded like it was coming from the room at the end of the corridor.

As Sarah approached, the voices were getting louder and louder. At first, she thought she would be finding a couple of the older kids arguing but she was surprised to find that it was actually two parents having a heated exchange of words with the teacher. The students were not in the classroom and the door was slightly cracked, allowing the sound to travel down the corridor.

The teacher was standing in front of the first rows of seats and the parents were standing almost too close to her, invading her space. The teacher was Mrs. Fowler, one of the less communicative ones, a willowy, skittish sort. Sarah recognized her from saying hello to her in the teacher's lounge, but they had never actually talked. The parents also looked familiar. Sarah remembered them now. They were the executive-looking couple that she had seen going into Mr. Coles' office on the day that her father had gone into hospital. Their daughter was one of Sarah's students. So what were they arguing about? Did they have another child in the sixth grade?

"Our son is a wonderful boy," the father was saying, "and there is no way that he would lie about something like that."

"I'm not sure you understand," the teacher said, with blushed cheeks and holding a folder firmly across her chest in the form of a shield.

"I can't believe you are wasting our time in this way," the mother said, raising her voice even further, "we are busy professionals. We should be at work right now and instead we are here talking about a computer glitch."

"It's not a glitch," the teacher said, adjusting her reading glasses and clutching her folder even tighter with her eyes cast down to the floor.

"Oh, please. Give me a break!" exclaimed the father, running his fingers through the top of his hair in frustration.

137

On impulse, Sarah knocked on the door. Pretending she hadn't heard a thing, she smiled and waved to the couple.

"Sorry to interrupt, Mrs. Fowler," Sarah said, "can I ask you a quick question? It won't be a minute, I promise."

The parents turned around abruptly, irritated by the intrusion, but then they recognized Sarah. Mrs. Fowler excused herself and walked to the door. Sarah gently pulled her to the corridor and closed the door behind her, out of earshot of the parents.

"Is everything all right?" Sarah said, "it's none of my business but I just overheard…"

"No, I'm glad you interrupted," Mrs. Fowler said, "I'm completely stressed out. I can't believe I'm having this problem with 6th grade kids. Do you know this couple?"

"Their daughter is in my class," Sarah nodded.

"Well, their son Mickey is in mine," Mrs. Fowler, "and he's turning into a handful really quickly, and they are determined to ignore it. If they don't do something now they are going to have a big problem on their hands in five-year's time."

"What did he do?" Sarah asked.

"Plagiarism," Mrs. Fowler said, "and he's not even eleven yet. I let it slide the first time but now it's obvious that he's just copying and pasting text straight from the Internet on his writing assignments. But they won't hear of it, they said their son said he didn't, and he never lies. Do they think he is just precocious, writing with the style of a thirty year old? They are completely blind. I've had it. I'm going to turn this over to Mr. Coles."

"I'm sorry you are stressed, Mrs. Fowler," Sarah said, " but let me know if there's anything I can do."

"Actually," Mrs. Fowler said, with a hint of amusement in her eyes, "you might be able to help."

"How?" Sarah said.

"What about your QC program?" Mrs. Fowler asked.

"To enroll them, you mean?" Sarah said, "I can bring you a leaflet."

"No, I don't mean that," she said, "Although we can offer them that later. I mean the four…. things…whatever you call them. Do you want to try them?"

"The four pillars? Right now?" Sarah said.

"Your class is out on the field trip, right?" Mrs. Fowler said, "mine are back in twenty minutes so we don't have much time."

Sarah was pleased that Mrs. Fowler had thought of her program, but on the other hand the four pillars were not designed to be a quick fix that could be implemented on the fly, like changing a flat tire. Sarah hesitated for an instant. Then she remembered Mrs. Lee's words. If there was to be progress, it was up to her to become the agent for change.

"Ok," Sarah said, "why not?"

Sarah entered the classroom with confidence and asked the parents if they wouldn't mind participating in an experiment from the QC program. She committed to keep the entire conversation to less than fifteen minutes. They both agreed and Sarah wrote the four pillars on the board as the parents and Mrs. Fowler took their seats on the front row. Starting with pillar one, the parents went first, and the teacher went second—establishing their facts and their concerns. The other party listened without interrupting. Then they each took turns asking questions.

At this point, it was clear that the temperature of the argument had gone down a few degrees and both parties were able to express themselves in less emotional terms. Mrs. Fowler had even let go of her folder and had both hands resting easily on her lap. By the time they had exchanged feedback from pillar number three and then were silent for a few moments for pillar four, Sarah realized that both sides of the argument had more in common than they thought.

When they spoke again, the parents said that they now understood that there was no possible way that their son Mickey had written the text in question once they realized the amount of care that Mrs. Fowler had put into double-checking this before bringing the matter to them. Mrs. Fowler in turn apologized for getting impatient, as she was aware of the difficulties that working parents face when supervising their child's homework and the time constraints they face.

"Besides," said the father, smiling now, "even though my wife and I are both professional auditors and work with computers, Mickey at his age is already much better at the computer than both of us put together. It's hard to follow what he's doing."

After exchanging possible solutions, the parents agreed to have a serious talk with Mickey about copying from others. They would also move Mickey's computer from his bedroom to the family room where it would be in plain view, which was generally advised anyway to allow parents to monitor their children's internet usage and protect them from online predators. They also agreed to take turns to get more involved with Mickey's schoolwork.

140

"I'll alert you immediately if I notice anything again," said Mrs. Fowler, "although I suspect that once Mickey realizes that his teacher and his parents are working together, he may not need any more dissuasion."

The parents said goodbye and left and Mrs. Fowler gently placed her hand on Sarah's back.

"You're on to something with that QC business of yours," Mrs. Fowler said, and winked, "thanks for saving the day."

"I'm starting to feel like a superhero," Sarah laughed.

Sarah loved the shorter days in midwinter when you could start to feel the season changing with the imperceptible few minutes' extra daylight as the days grew longer. She first noticed this as she got home from school on Friday in the way that the sun was reflecting on the kitchen counter at a slightly deeper angle, which gave the room a golden hue and reminded her of winter in the apple orchard back home. She decided to call Tom right away to clear any misunderstanding of the day before. At this time he was probably still at work. Sure enough, the voicemail picked up her call. Tom's greeting was crisp and professional, just what you would expect from someone in the corporate world. Sarah didn't leave a message. She would try again later. Not twenty seconds went by before Tom called her back.

"Hi Sarah," he said, "were you trying to reach me?"

"That was quick!" she said.

"I'm glad you called," Tom said, "listen, I just wanted to clarify about yesterday. I don't know what the deal is with Amberlee, but I got the impression that you weren't comfortable with finding me there. She just sent me an email earlier in the week, asking if I could help set up at your house, because you were organizing an event at your school and you would be running tight on time. I assumed that you had asked her to contact me, and that you were aware that I would be helping out. It was my fault to assume, but I never thought to ask."

"It's understandable to assume that I knew," Sarah said, "and thanks for doing it, particularly as you have such a busy job."

"Hey, I had to rearrange a meeting, but I'm happy to do it for you, Sarah," his tone become a bit more purposeful, "I want you to know that you can call me, anytime. Anytime."

"Thanks, Tom," Sarah said, "I appreciate it. Please don't feel bad. I'm sure Amberlee just forgot to tell me."

"I don't know about that," Tom said, "Can I be frank with you?"

"Go ahead."

"In my business it is important to call it like I see it. That's what I get paid to do and I am pretty good at it. As a consultant I come in from the outside and see things in a perspective that the business owner is not aware of. So I'll give you my consulting eye on this one. I don't think Amberlee forgot to tell you; I think she arranged it so that I would be there with her alone. Don't get me wrong, I'm flattered, but there's nothing going on as far as I'm concerned. It's just that I don't like the fact that I was blindsided."

"Of course," Sarah said, "if you are right, then Amberlee should apologize both to me and to you."

142

"And there's one more thing," Tom said, "I'm not entirely innocent."

"How do you mean?"

"In part, I agreed to help out because the meeting was at your home and I thought you and I would have a chance to chat a bit before the rest of the group arrived."

"Not that innocent, huh?" Sarah laughed, feeling her cheeks flush.

She sat on the kitchen counter, letting the sunlight wash over her as the conversation with Tom flowed easily. They talked about his work, about Sarah's after-school program. Tom confessed that he had originally joined the book club to please his mother, who was worried that he was working too hard and had insisted that he have some sort of social life outside of work, even if it was just for one day a month. The sun disappeared behind the trees as Sarah stayed where she was, listening to Tom talk about his other passion, cooking, and his plans to open a bistro.

"Do you know what I just realized?' Sarah said, "I'm very lucky. You are working on a job that you do well just so that you can get to the point where you can open your restaurant and indulge in your passion for food, but I am already working on the job that is my passion."

"And you have a talent for it, as well," Tom said.

"That remains to be seen," Sarah said.

"I think that the fact that you were given such a responsibility in your debut year speaks for itself."

"Thank you," Sarah said, "that's very kind."

"Here's something you should know, Sarah," Tom said, "I never say something just to be kind. I am brutally honest. It comes with the territory. If I don't think it's appropriate to say what I think I may choose to remain silent, but I'll never say something I don't mean."

"You give real feedback," Sarah said, "that's valuable."

"Exactly," Tom said, "and here's my feedback. The sooner you realize that you have a special talent for what you are doing, and the sooner you own up to it, the better for you, your students, and your after-school program. There's no point in being overly humble. I don't mean you need to be arrogant, but you do need to be assertive. You are in a position of leadership, and you owe it to everyone involved to take that responsibility and step up to the plate. You are no regular new teacher. Your principal knows it; your colleagues seem to know it. It seems that you are the only one who doesn't know it yet. It's nothing to be wary of. Quite the contrary. Who knows why we are made the way we are? What gives you that particular ability? It's not something that you actively seek out; it's just the way it is. Even Amberlee mentioned it."

"She did?"

"Yes," Tom said, "I don't remember her words exactly, but it didn't sound like she was particularly tickled about it. She said something about all this attention being centered on you before you had a chance to prove yourself. I think she was worried that you may be overstretched and that people were piling unreasonable expectations on you. Anyway, that's just my take. As I said, I tell it as I see it."

"Some food for thought right there," Sarah said.

She knew she was going to have a conversation with Amberlee, but in her heart she didn't feel like tackling it

144

right now. She would let the weekend drift along without thinking about it. It would clear her mind, and on Monday she would decide how to best approach Amberlee. Saturday was filled with errands, cleaning the apartment, and grocery shopping. A leisurely Sunday morning led to an afternoon of reading, watching old movies, and slow cooking a beef stew with her mother's recipe.

By Monday Sarah felt restored, energized, and ready to face the week when her Quality Conversations after-school program officially started. The only cloud in the horizon was seeing Amberlee at work. While the weekend had indeed renewed her energy, it had not given her any further insight into how she would approach Amberlee, but it had to be done. So at lunchtime Sarah went into the teacher's lounge hoping to find Amberlee there. She saw her in a corner, eating a sandwich with one hand and absently thumbing through a magazine with the other.

"Hey Amberlee," Sarah said, "I'd like to talk to you about something. Can I buy you a cup of coffee in the cafeteria?"

"Oh, I was going to make a couple of phone calls," Amberlee said.

"How about if I throw in a slice of blueberry pie with the coffee?"

"How can I say no to that!" Amberlee said.

They both walked to the cafeteria, idly chatting about the weekend. They sat down to two cups of coffee and shared a slice of pie.

"So?' Amberlee said, "What did you want to talk about?"

"The book club meeting, on Thursday," Sarah said.

"It went great, didn't it? Amberlee said, "You don't need to thank me; I did it because I wanted to. I told you it was going to be fine."

"It was more than fine," Sarah said, "I appreciate your help. I really do. You worked really hard and we all had such a nice time." Sarah paused. "That's why it's a bit difficult to say what I'm about to say."

"What's wrong?"

"I spoke to Tom," Sarah said.

Amberlee looked down and blew into her coffee cup.

"About what?" she said, without looking up.

"There seemed to be a misunderstanding," Sarah said, "I didn't know you had asked him to come over to my house early to help set up. He thought I knew and that I would be there."

"So?"

"I would have preferred it if you told me," Sarah said, "then there would have been no misunderstanding."

"It was no misunderstanding. I arranged it so that I'd have a chance to see Tom for a little bit before you all arrived. Is that a crime?"

"No crime," Sarah said, "I just wish you would have told me. It took me by surprise."

"You would have disapproved," Amberlee said, "that's why I didn't tell you. You would have thought it was desperate and you would have tried to talk me out of it."

"Is that how you see me?' Sarah said, "As a judgmental bore?"

146

"Well?" Amberlee asked, "What would you have said if I had asked you?"

Sarah thought for a moment. She didn't know what made her more upset, the lie or the implication that she couldn't be trusted to understand a friend.

"I would have probably said that it wasn't a good idea," Sarah said.

"There you go then," Amberlee said.

"That doesn't mean that you were right not to tell me."

There was a long silence, until Amberlee spoke again.

"So when did you speak to Tom?" she asked.

"Friday evening," Sarah replied.

"So you must have been thinking about this all weekend," she said, "did you plan this conversation? How you would apply your famous four pillars to me?"

Sarah didn't reply. She did not like the direction the conversation was taking, and she didn't want to let her emotions get the better of her.

"So are you seeing Tom now?" Amberlee said, "is that what you wanted to tell me?"

"Oh, now that's uncalled for," Sarah said.

"Well, you were right," she said, "is that what you wanted to hear? Yes, it wasn't a good idea. As soon as Tom got there it was obvious that he expected you to be home and that he was uncomfortable and not interested in asking me out or talking to me about anything except how remarkable you are. So that's how it went. Me hoping he would ask me on a date and him hoping that you would arrive soon. Pretty sad, right? So there. You were right. Happy?"

Amberlee got up and left without another word, not allowing Sarah a chance to reply. Sarah stayed there, drinking her coffee, waiting for her pulse to stop racing. At first she thought that she might had been too harsh on Amberlee. She obviously cared about Tom and was hurt that he didn't return her feelings. The conversation kept replaying in her head. It finally struck her. It wasn't that she cared so much about what Amberlee had said. More than anything it was the fact that she had attempted a quality conversation and had failed. She was supposed to be the one to show the way for others, and here she was—speechless—stumped by a simple difference of opinion with a friend.

The professional in her was struggling to identify where it had all gone wrong. She had asked questions, she had listened, she had provided feedback, and she was now reflecting. What else could she have done?

Then she remembered how Amberlee had referred to "her famous four pillars" in a mocking manner. Sarah had counted Amberlee as one of her allies, but it was clear that she was not onboard. Was this what Mrs. Lee and Mr. Coles had warned her about? Could this be just Amberlee's way of displaying her resistance to change? Or was this personal? She couldn't help remembering what Tom had said. Maybe he was right. He must be a pretty good judge of character to make a good consultant. She left the cafeteria and headed back to her classroom. Just before the students arrived back from their lunch break Mr. Coles assistant stopped by to see Sarah.

"Just wanted to let you know, Sarah," she said, "the response to the intro session was more than expected.

We'll have to assign the QC program to the bigger room after all."

"That's great," Sarah said, "thanks for letting me know."

"If I can help you with anything else, just let me know," she said, "I'm really looking forward to the program."

This was just what Sarah needed to hear. People had signed up, they were looking forward to the program, and there was an excitement in the air about it. For the rest of the afternoon as she threw herself into her work, Sarah was able to push back any thoughts of the conversation with Amberlee. As soon as she was home, however, the bad taste returned. At that moment, Sarah knew what she had to do.

The first session of the after-school program started without a hitch, except for the notable absence of Amberlee. Sarah had not seen her since her outburst at the cafeteria. But the participants seemed to be in high spirits, as Margie with her natural authority helped get everyone settled and introduced Sarah, and then took a seat at the back of the room. Sarah started off with a simple icebreaker game. She asked everyone in the room to turn to the person on the left, introduce themselves, and tell whatever they could about themselves in thirty seconds. The room was instantly alight with conversation. At the end of the thirty seconds, she told people to switch roles and introduce themselves to the person on their right. When the time was up, Sarah pointed to the lady who was sitting on Margie's left.

149

"Please tell us everything you learned about the person on your right, but tell it to us in the first person, as if it was you."

"Oh no!" the lady said, looking at Margie and breaking into a fit of giggles, "I don't remember anything."

"Come on," Sarah prodded, "at least you must remember their name?"

"Yes, her name is Margie," the lady began, then corrected, "I mean, *my* name is Margie."

"Great," Sarah said, "that's a start. What else?"

Thinking hard, the lady managed to contain her giggles.

"OK, my name is Margie," she said, "I teach the fourth grade here at Jackson. Oh, I'm the grade-level chair. I am in the same grade as you, Sarah, actually."

"That's right," Sarah said, "excellent!'

"And…" the lady looked at Margie again, "I have three grown daughters…"

Margie nodded, encouraging the lady to continue.

"This is hard!" the lady said, "if I had known I would have paid more attention!"

They all laughed.

"Wait, I remember something else," the lady said, "I have a dog called Bruce, named after my favorite musician, Bruce Springsteen."

Even Sarah joined in the laughter this time; it was not easy to picture Margie as a fan of rock music.

"Thank you very much," Sarah said to the lady, and then looked at Margie, "so, tell us, how did she do? Did she get you correctly?"

"Absolutely," Margie said, and shook her neighbor's hand, "good job."

"Was there any other information that you shared with her but got left out?"

"Yes," Margie said, "I mentioned my husband's occupation, that I enjoy gardening, and a couple of other things."

"Great," Sarah said, "thanks Margie."

Then Sarah instructed everybody to turn to the person on their right and relate back to them what they remembered about that they had said about themselves. Once again the room was bursting with voices, but this time there were palpable pauses as people were struggling to remember. When the time was up, everyone was beginning to understand the point of the game.

"So now we know a little more about each other," Sarah said, "and more importantly we know that it is not so easy to really listen to someone with our full attention. Before I shared with you what this exercise was about, we were all listening with our ears, but we were probably still thinking of other things at the same time: what we were going to fix for dinner, the errands we need to run tomorrow, and things like that. There is a running commentary in our heads that is not that easy to quiet down. We think we are listening, it looks like we are listening, but our minds are not fully connected in the moment. This takes us to the first pillar of *Quality Conversations*: Active Listening."

By now Sarah had everyone's full attention with people in active listening mode. The rest of the session went by quickly as the audience participated by asking questions and contributing examples from their own lives.

"Ok, that's all we have time for today," Sarah said, "but there's no reason that this quality conversation has to stop here. I invite you to take this home with you and share it with your family and with your friends, and practice your listening skills. We will be learning more about this next time. Thank you all so much for making this first session so easy for me, and I look forward to seeing you next week."

As the room cleared, Margie approached Sarah and helped her lock up.

"That was really good, Sarah," Margie said, "it's incredible to think that this is the first time you've done something like this."

"Thanks Margie!" Sarah said, "you have no idea how much your words mean to me. I am just finding my feet."

"Well, you certainly found them," Margie said, "and you hit the ground running."

Sarah floated on the success of the first day. As she got home, she reached for her mobile phone to call Mrs. Lee and share the excitement and thank her for all her help. There was a text message waiting.

"How did it go?" It was from Tom. Sarah was pleased that he had remembered.

Consolation

Sarah leaned back on her favorite apple tree, the lawn still damp from a passing sprinkle of spring rain. The voices of her mother and her sister wafted over as they sat knitting on the porch. She could hear snippets of their easy conversation. Their words floated in and out of her attention and allowed her mind to wander. The first few sessions of the after-school program had gone well as Sarah became more and more confident in her leadership role. By the time spring break rolled around, Sarah took the opportunity to make a quick visit home, eager to see Gayle's growing bump.

When she thought back to the first couple of weeks in her new job, Sarah found it hard to believe how far she had come in just a matter of months. That it had been an eventful time was an understatement. The program had grown and solidified. Even more people were trying to sign up once it was under way and word got out that it was *the* program to attend. She had become a minor celebrity in her school. Sometimes parents recognized her in the street or at the grocery store, and came up to her to thank her for her work. *Quality Conversations* was quickly becoming something that people were taking into their homes and into their workplace. It was more than Sarah could have imagined.

153

The only one cloud in her horizon was Amberlee. After her reaction about that evening with Tom and the book club, Sarah had found it hard to seek her company or have any sort of conversation with her. This had only added to the awkward tension.

"What's the matter Sarah?" her mother called out from the porch.

Sarah shaded her eyes to look at them. They had stopped knitting and were looking at her.

"You were looking so relaxed with your eyes closed and suddenly you twitched and frowned," Gayle said, teasing.

"Oh, I was just thinking of something," Sarah said.

"Work?" Gayle said.

"No, actually, work is going great," Sarah replied, "it's a friend I'm having a little trouble with."

"I want to know everything," Gayle said, "spill it out."

"Come inside and help me get dinner started," her mother said, "and you can chat in there."

As they were going inside, Sarah heard her mobile phone ring. She rushed to her handbag to get it but the voice mail service picked up before she could reach it. She listened to the message and put the phone back in her bag.

"That's odd," she said to herself as she went back to the kitchen to join the other two women.

"What is odd?" Gayle asked, handing her the peeler and a bowl of vegetables.

"There was a message from the National Afterschool Association," Sarah said, "to confirm if I would be available to speak at the conference in Phoenix."

"What?" Gayle said, "that's fantastic, Sis!"

154

"I think there must be a mistake," Sarah said, "I remember Mr. Coles mentioned the conference as something I might want to attend, but how would I be a speaker? I'm a newbie!"

"Being a newbie hasn't stopped you before," Gayle said.

"I'm sure it's nothing," Sarah said.

"So when is it?" Gayle said, "take me to Phoenix with you!"

"I don't know yet," Sarah said, "besides, you'll have your baby by then. You'll have your hands full."

"Oh, reality…" Gayle sighed, "it's highly overrated. Anyway. Tell me what you were frowning about before the phone rang. That friend. And spare no details. And keep peeling; Mom has the pastry ready."

"Ah, yes," Sarah said, "Amberlee."

Sarah busied herself peeling carrots and potatoes for a chicken potpie, as she retold her mother and Gayle all of her misgivings about Amberlee's behavior. Sarah played down the part about Tom; she didn't want to give her excitable sister the wrong impression.

"It's simple," Gayle said, "she's jealous of you. I would be jealous too. You come in, fresh from college, and while she is doing a reasonably job as a new teacher, you become this wunderkind that everyone is gushing about. Very annoying."

"Who's annoying?" said Noah, peeking his head in as he finished his work in the barn,

"Sarah," Gayle said, "a friend is jealous of her."

Gayle pulled Noah to the window seat and sat on his knee. She gave him a summarized version of the conver-

155

sation, while he tenderly patted her swelling stomach. In the fading amber sunshine coming through the window, they were both glowing with happiness. *This is what it's all about,* Sarah thought, *we live for moments like this.* Noah seemed to have acquired a new confidence, a solid assurance, ever since knowing he was becoming a father.

"There may be more to it," Noah said simply.

Sarah paid attention to Noah; he had a keen sense for the undercurrents of what makes people tick.

"What do you think it is, then, Noah?" Sarah said.

"Well," Noah said, "I don't know your friend, but I would say there is something she is not telling you."

"Well, of course," Gayle said, "she wouldn't tell Sarah that she is jealous of her, would she?"

"I mean something that has nothing to do with Sarah," Noah said, "something that's eating at her. Just my guess. I could be wrong."

"I think I'll ask her," Sarah said, "it's worth a try."

"So how's it going otherwise?" Noah asked.

"It's quite amazing," Sarah said.

In the retelling of the last few weeks, something suddenly clicked in her. All the elements that had come together to make her first big project at work such a success became crisp and clear. Mr. Coles, the after-school program, Margie, Amy and Ed, Mrs. Lee. As Sarah was telling them about the sessions at the after-school program, her father arrived and they all sat around the table for dinner. They kept asking questions about the school and the program. They felt they had participated, in a way,

156

over the holidays with the homework assignment testing the four pillars in practice.

"I was teasing you earlier," Gayle said, "but really, Sarah, you seem so much happier. I remember at Thanksgiving you were almost ready to quit, and now you are all lit up with excitement. I'm a bit jealous."

"Jealous? What for?"

"Well, I have everything I ever wished for, my husband, my baby on the way. Don't get me wrong," Gayle said, "but I see you working on such interesting things, meeting such interesting people, it makes my world feel small in comparison."

"Don't be silly," her father said, "I bet Sarah makes it look easier than it is."

"Well, it's not easy all the time," Sarah said, "but the parents and teachers have been wonderful and I couldn't have done it without your support. I want to thank you all."

"You're welcome," said Gayle, smiling with satisfaction, "there, we helped a little then."

"Enormously," said Sarah, "and most particularly you, Noah, you were the first person who got me started on this path. You are a natural!"

"Me?" Noah said, blood rushing to his cheeks, "I didn't do anything special."

"You're blushing honey!" Gayle said, laughing, and planted a tender kiss on his shoulder.

The Unspoken Words

First things first. As soon as Sarah got back to her apartment from her spring break trip, she knew that she didn't want to delay it any further. The next dinner at the pizza place with Amberlee was supposed to happen some time ago, but Amberlee had not called or spoken to Sarah beyond a passing hello in the teacher's lounge. Sarah decided to take matters into her own hands and sent a message to Amberlee's phone. She wrote simply, "We need to talk."

Amberlee didn't reply immediately, but later that day, Sarah found a note on her locker, saying, "Pizza tonight at 7:00 p.m."

The ambience at the pizza restaurant was upbeat as ever. It was an uplifting experience every time she went there, but tonight Sarah was not feeling entirely at ease. What she had prepared to say to Amberlee was not pleasant but it needed to be said. She made herself relax by thinking of the pleasure of browsing around in the bookstore after their dinner. She expected it would be quite a brief dinner this time, probably no dessert. Amberlee

159

arrived carrying some shopping bags and with her hair freshly cut and styled. She had also had it colored a deeper shade of chestnut, as if she was gradually trying to get away from her red natural coloring.

"Your hair looks wonderful!" Sarah said.

"Thanks!" Amberlee said, plopping in her chair, obviously tired.

"Have you been shopping?"

"Madly," Amberlee said, and opened the shopping bags slightly so Sarah could take a look inside.

There was a pair of sandals, one bag with several pieces of lingerie from a well-known brand, a chiffon top with sparkly sequins and a skirt.

"Wow!" Sarah said, "good taste."

"You're not saying what you're thinking," Amberlee said.

Sarah paused, then smiled, "You're right. I'm thinking that you've spent quite a bit of money there."

"Yes," Amberlee said, "I went a little crazy."

"Don't let me spoil your fun," Sarah said, "it's none of my business."

"Yes it is," Amberlee said, "you're my critical peer, aren't you?"

The server came over to take their order. When he left, Sarah took the opportunity to jump straight into what she was here to say.

"Amberlee," she said, "about the other day at the cafeteria."

"I know, I'm so sorry," Amberlee said, "I got carried away, and I shouldn't have let time go by without apologizing. I behaved like a spoiled brat."

"Apology accepted," Sarah said, "but that's not really what I was saying. The fact is that it made me think about this arrangement to be critical peers. It seems to me that sometimes you tell me what you think I want to hear, and then what you really think ends up coming out the wrong way. I think you are having trouble with the concept of *Quality Conversations*, you are not really onboard, and it's better if we don't force this situation. I don't want to push anything down your throat, but on the other hand, I am putting a lot of myself into this effort and I need support. And well…I need a critical peer but I also sometimes just need a cheerleader."

Amberlee looked down into her plate for a few moments. Finally she blew her hair away from her face and wrapped her fingers firmly around her water glass.

"You may have a point," Amberlee said, "but it's not what you think. I am struggling with the four pillars, but not because I am not supporting your efforts. I am actually frustrated because I believe that the pillars do work."

"I don't understand," Sarah said.

Their pizzas arrived, and the meal that Sarah expected to be short lasted for much longer than any of their previous conversations. Once Amberlee opened her heart there was no stopping the flood of her repressed worry, her emotions, her confusion at the situation that had developed in her family. Her parents had formed one of the most solid marriages she had ever known, and suddenly they had decided to separate. Amberlee related to Sarah the details of their divorce, how they were now fighting over every single penny in their savings accounts, over

161

every item of furniture, over who kept the dog, over who would continue to see which set of friends.

Her father had been caught in an indiscretion with a woman he met at his golf club and her mother would not forgive him. The woman in question had actually been in their home as a dinner guest, and this was a humiliation that Amberlee's mother could not tolerate. Her father denied everything and her mother blamed everything on him. In each of their petty arguments and battles, they were using Amberlee as the linchpin to deliver messages and ultimatums to each other. They were destroying the person they loved the most, their own daughter, and they couldn't stop themselves.

"Oh, Amberlee, I'm so sorry," Sarah said, "I had no idea you were going through all this."

Sarah thought back to Noah's words. He had guessed right; there had been something eating up at Amberlee. How did Noah sense these things?

"I didn't want to say anything at first," Amberlee said, "I guess I thought it would sort itself out, somehow, as if talking about it made it real. You always think these things happen to other people; it's very surreal when it happens to you," Amberlee said, her eyes red with repressed tears, "but in fact it happens to anybody. I'm exhausted. It's no excuse for my behavior though, but I just didn't know how to deal with it and I snapped at you. I feel pulled in all directions. They are using me as their punching bag; they tell me things I wish I had never known."

"What do you mean?" Sarah said.

162

"My father said that they were about to separate when my mother found out that she was expecting me, and that she tried to…." Amberlee pressed her lips together to stop them quivering.

Why would anybody say something like that to their daughter? Sarah could not understand the motivation, but then when emotions are allowed to go wild and take control of the communication, any sense of right or wrong goes out the window.

"He probably didn't mean anything he said," Sarah said, "they are not thinking straight."

"All these years and I never knew that they didn't even like each other," Amberlee said.

"I'm sure that's not the case," Sarah said, "they are united in their love for you."

"I know I'm an adult and lots of people get a divorce," Amberlee said, "but this really hit me hard. I can't help it. I remember reading Hansel and Gretel and thinking that was the most horrifying thing that could happen to you. It was the sheer terror of being abandoned, cast away from the security of your family and your home. That's how I feel. It's tearing me apart."

The pizza led to dessert, then to cups of herbal tea, and then cappuccinos. The crowd was thinning at the restaurant and they realized that they must have been talking for hours.

"I guess we better go. These guys must be getting ready to close." Amberlee said, signaling for the check, and reaching over to touch Sarah's hand. "Thanks for listening."

163

"Anytime," Sarah said, reaching for her wallet.

Amberlee refused to let her pay and firmly handed her own credit card with the bill.

"It's on me," Amberlee said, "the least I can do. Please let me."

"Thank you very much. I'll accept graciously then," Sarah said, putting away her wallet, then shaking her head softly, "so all this time when we have been talking about quality conversations, you were in the middle of this violent war of words."

"Exactly," Amberlee said, "I have been trying to tell them both about the four pillars but there is no way on earth that they will listen to reason. So I spend too much money shopping and change the color of my hair instead," she said with a wry smile.

"Sometimes a girl needs to shop," Sarah shrugged, "I'll help you return those tomorrow."

"And my hair is too dark," Amberlee said.

"Your color will come back," Sarah said.

"You are a good friend, Sarah," Amberlee said, "and I've treated you unkindly. All that nonsense about Tom. Playground stuff."

"Forgotten," Sarah said.

"By the way, if you want to go out with him, you have my blessing. He seems like a really nice guy, funny and good looking."

Back at work on Monday morning, Sarah called back the number for the Afterschool Association. A polite voice asked her to please hold as she located the person who had left her the message. After about a minute or so, an energetic voice picked up.

"Sarah?" the voice said, "this is Debbie. Thanks for calling me back."

"I think there must be a mistake," Sarah said, "I'm a new teacher at Jackson, not one of your speakers."

"Let me check," Debbie said, "let's see, OK, here you are. Sarah Granger, Jackson Elementary in Dallas. I have your home and mobile numbers here."

She repeated Sarah's numbers.

"Is this information correct?" she asked.

"Yes, the details are correct," Sarah said, "but I'm a little confused."

"It says here your presentation would be about the *Four Pillars of Quality Conversations.*"

"That's my program," Sarah said.

"Did you get the package yet?" she asked.

"No."

"I see," she said, "don't worry. I've just sent them a few days ago. If you don't get it by next week, call me back and I'll send another one. You have all the details there, schedule, accommodation, the tentative list of speakers. We are now trying to confirm the list; that's why I called you."

"Let me talk to my principal and get back to you," Sarah said.

"Absolutely," Debbie said, "and feel free to call with any questions."

Mr. Coles was in his office, and his assistant waved Sarah to go right in. Mr. Coles had his back to the door,

165

leaning down to pick up a thick manila envelope that had spilled its contents on the floor. The door was wide open so Sarah knocked on the doorframe.

"Mr. Coles," Sarah said, "do you have a minute?"

"Come in Sarah!" Mr. Coles said, pulling himself up, "just the person I needed to see. You must be psychic. I was coming over to see you right this minute."

He turned around and tucked the information back inside the envelope and handed it over to Sarah.

"Look at that!" Mr. Coles said, "I'm so proud I could burst!"

Sarah saw the letterhead of the National Afterschool Association and didn't need to read any further. She knew what was inside.

"So it wasn't a mistake then," she said, and laughed, "they called me to confirm if I would be available, and I thought they'd got the wrong person."

"Well, who else could it be?" Mr. Coles said, "it's your program."

"But I am so new at all this," Sarah said.

"I think I've heard that before," Mr. Coles said.

"I know. I keep saying the same thing over and over. It's just that it's happening so quickly."

"I'm the first one to admit it," he said, "it did take me by surprise. They called a couple of weeks ago out of the blue to ask me my opinion about the program, so I wrote them an email and attached a few copies of the participants' evaluations and my own. The next thing I know, they sent me this invitation to hand over to you."

166

"It's incredible," Sarah said, "I'm both thrilled and maybe a little nervous."

"Well, new or not, they want you to speak at the conference, and I am in full support. It's a wonderful program, it has had such a positive response, and it's the least we can do to share our experience with other schools."

"How do you think they heard about the program?" Sarah asked, "it's not like it's been going on for all that long."

"I didn't think to ask," Mr. Coles said, "maybe it's related to my report. In one of my reports, I mentioned the QC program and recommended it to be considered for a countywide roll out. Maybe that's how?"

"Maybe," Sarah said, "but news sure traveled fast."

"You could ask the organizers," Mr. Coles said, "they'll tell you how they got your name. I'm very glad they did."

"Thank you Mr. Coles," Sarah said, "I'll accept, of course, and I'll need your help to prepare. I've never done anything like this before."

"Piece of cake," Mr. Coles said, clapping his hands together and smiling, "it's just like the after-school program, only you are talking to thousands of people instead of dozens."

"OK," Sarah covered her face with her hands, "now I'm officially nervous."

"And another thing," Mr. Coles said, "they'll probably tell you when they send you the speakers' package but they like to have a paper on the subject, so that participants can download it from the website if they are interested in knowing more in advance of the conference."

"Do you know how long it usually is?" Sarah asked.

167

"It depends on the subject. I think they leave it up to the speaker," he said.

❧

The last few months before the end of the school year were here. Sarah couldn't believe that already her first year as a teacher was almost over; time had gone by in a swirl of activity. Her initial resolution not to neglect her social life had gone by the wayside. The only outside activity that she had kept up was the book club, with the comforting thought that Tom was always there. Their growing friendship felt safe and familiar—talking about literature and reading, sharing a lovely time without any impositions, and letting the future unfold at its own pace.

Her work had taken over every waking hour. When she was not teaching, grading, or preparing lessons, she was fully immersed in the after-school QC program or the preparation for her guest speaking appearance at the conference. She had never attended one of these conferences, so she threw herself into preparing as much as possible ahead of time. The more polished the presentation, the more confidence she would have as a speaker. The after-school program was rolling along nicely. Sarah had already introduced the four pillars, developed role-playing games, exercises, examples, and had gathered feedback from the participants. There was already a waitlist in place for a second QC program. The future was full of promise. It could not have been more all-round successful.

This morning Sarah went through her morning routine and realized that things that used to require her attention had now become second nature. Even the smallest details, the porcelain mug with her name on it, her locker decorated with pictures drawn by the students, her satchel bag stacked full with the graded homework, it all felt familiar and purposeful. Today would be a particularly long day, with parent-teacher meetings probably running straight into early evening, depending on the turnout.

While some of the teachers were not looking forward to meeting the parents and saw their role as teachers as independent from the parenting role, Sarah was eager to share with the parents their children's achievements and challenges. She strongly believed that the work in the classroom would only be as strong as the link she managed to establish between the school and the environment at home. Sometimes a word from the parents would give an invaluable insight into a particular obstacle that a student was experiencing that would take weeks for a teacher to figure out in isolation. So it was in this spirit that, after a full day in the classroom, Sarah headed back out of the teacher's lounge to her classroom after a short break to welcome the parents. It was probably because things were running so smoothly that what happened next took her by surprise.

The executive couple, the parents that were having a disagreement with Mrs. Fowler when Sarah had stepped in to help, were sitting opposite her now talking about their daughter. Sarah had no concerns to report; their daughter was an average student with good discipline.

"If I could say anything at all," Sarah said, "it would be to encourage her to participate a little bit more in class."

169

"About that," the mother said, "I've had a concern now for a couple of months."

"I don't know that I would call it a concern," the father said.

"Please feel free to tell me," Sarah said, "that's what I'm here for, to help your daughter have the best possible educational experience."

"It's not so much about our daughter," the mother said, "it's about you, Miss Granger."

There followed a short pause that felt like an ocean of silence to Sarah.

"We know this is your first year," the mother continued, "and overall we are really pleased with how things are going, but we feel that all this talk about your after-school program has taken on such a prominent place now in the school that we feel that you may be neglecting the work in the classroom. Mrs. Fowler said that last year at this same time they were a couple of lessons further ahead."

Sarah felt her ears get hot. What had just happened? Was this real? As if time had been suspended, Sarah stared at the specks of dust floating in the golden sun in the fading afternoon sun. She wished she could ride on that ray of light all the way to her parent's farm, all the way to her favorite apple tree. She traced the specks of dust on the desk, drawing a circle with her finger. The thoughts that rushed through her head in one instant could have filled pages and pages of text.

All that hard work, those long days preparing, the long nights revising and rethinking. The love and passion that she put into her work at the expense of her own private time.

170

Clichés flashed through her mind. *You can't please them all. You win some you lose some. You can bring a horse to water but you can't force it to drink.* And then, all at once, her thoughts become calm and focused, as if a cool breeze had cleared a swath of blue sky after a violent storm. No. She wouldn't let this pass. She objected to the position that these parents were taking, and she would let them know. Sarah waited until both parents had said their piece. Hanging in the silence, expecting her to reply, they were now both looking at her, growing less sure with every passing second.

"So, that is all that you are concerned about?" Sarah asked. They both nodded.

"Nothing else?" Sarah said. "Are you absolutely sure?"

They nodded again, less emphatically, and shuffled in their chairs.

"Well," Sarah said, "I listened to you attentively, and now I expect that you will pay me the same courtesy and listen to what I have to say. You have referred to the program of *Quality Conversations* as if that was something that occurs outside of the classroom. And it does, if you consider that parents and teachers meet in the after school program together with the students. But do not be fooled. The classroom is a conversation! There can be no learning without communication. If we expect students to listen; ask questions; give and receive feedback; and reflect, then we are asking them to follow the four pillars of quality conversations with their teachers!

Our first teacher is our mother, and I was lucky that my mother was a great communicator. She said to me that I would never be lost in this world, because I knew how to

171

find my way through communication. I wish every child had a mother like mine, but not everybody is that lucky. Many children grow into adults without ever experiencing the power of a truly open and productive conversation.

Do I care? Yes, absolutely. I may be new as a teacher, but I was born to enjoy talking, listening, and helping others. People gravitate to me because I listen and I am able to make them feel better about their situation, no matter what it is. I now realize that I didn't choose this after-school program. It chose me.

If I can help just one person, out of all of this, to find the way to *Quality Conversations*, then it is worth doing. I can say that it has already enriched my life beyond any possible expectation. I am grateful for this opportunity. I will fulfill my role with every fiber in my body; this is how much it means to me. If I were you, I would try to look at this as an opportunity for your children. Because not only do they have a chance to participate in the after-school program, and you as well, but because they are in my classroom."

Sarah could hardly believe her own ears, listening to her own voice produce this calm, confident, unassuming truth that was pouring out of her as if she had rehearsed it for the conference.

"When you are in my classroom," she continued, "you are in an environment that can influence your self-esteem, it can improve your emotional and intellectual development. I not only give out *Quality Conversations* in the program, I live it every day. I suspect that if I wasn't a teacher, I would be implementing something similar in a company, or a hospital, or wherever my destiny would have taken me.

172

As it happens, I am a teacher—a pretty good one—and I am engaging my students and empowering them to communicate effectively—a skill that will stay with them for the rest of their lives. Sure, they will have math, history, and geography, and they may forget eighty percent of it by the time they have kids of their own, but one thing that I am sure they will not forget is to have *Quality Conversations* with their own children, and their grandchildren after that. They will build stronger relationships and happier homes. Now let me ask you a question, regarding being behind schedule, did you ask your daughter to show you her class work? Did you compare it with the curriculum? Did you find anything lacking?"

Both parents were looking at Sarah as if in deep hypnosis, not quite sure how to reply or whether to reply at all. The father made an attempt.

"Occasionally we try to look at her work," he said, "but that is her mother usually, isn't it, honey?"

"Yes," she said, "when I can, of course, although nowadays we are both so busy that it's mostly the nanny. She picks them up from school until we get home. It's not easy with our schedule."

"Even if you have just a few minutes each day, you can make those minutes matter. Anyway. So you are just going by what Mrs. Fowler said?" Sarah asked.

"Well," the father said, and looked intently at his wife.

"It wasn't Mrs. Fowler directly," she said, "it just came up in conversation with one of the other teachers."

"Who?" Sarah said.

"I can't remember exactly," the wife was now blushing, "I didn't mean to upset you, Miss Granger, it was just something I thought I'd bring up."

"I'm glad you did," Sarah said, "and in the future, please feel free to ask me whenever you have a question about your child's education. The curriculum has been reshuffled since last year; it basically covers the same ground but the sequence of events has changed so they have covered lessons at the beginning of the year that are now interconnected with what we are seeing now. Mrs. Fowler may have been commenting on that and her comment may have been taken out of context. When I took over this year it was already in place; it has nothing to do with my appointment or the after-school program. By the way, the general opinion is that it makes more sense this way."

"Ah, we didn't know," the father said, "then it sounds like it was all just a silly misunderstanding."

After all the parents had left and the halls had cleared, Sarah still felt the energy from her speech to the couple. She felt so strongly about it that she decided to write down some of her own words. That is exactly the kind of confidence and passion that she needed to convey at the conference. She knew she had it in her, but now that it had bubbled up to the surface it made so much sense. *Quality Conversations* was such a natural fit for her, not just the way she naturally communicated, but the environment in which she had been brought up. In fact she couldn't think of any other teacher who would fit the role so well, except perhaps for Mrs. Lee. In one swift moment it had all solidified so clearly. What a difference a moment

174

can make. Sarah slung her satchel over her shoulder and closed the classroom door behind her and smiled to herself. Everything was so quiet after the students left. She felt a deep satisfying sense of home in her classroom. She loved her job. She was exactly where she was meant to be.

"Did it go well?" Mr. Coles called out, walking towards her as she turned into the corridor.

"Pretty good, yes," Sarah said.

"I could tell from your big smile," he said.

"Was I smiling?"

"More like grinning," he laughed, "by the way, what did you do to them?"

Mr. Coles nodded towards the couple of parents that Sarah had given her speech to, as they were getting into their car, the last ones to leave.

"Why?" Sarah said, "did they say something to you?"

"Something?" Mr. Coles said, "they couldn't stop gushing about you."

"Really?" she said.

"I was surprised because usually if they want to talk it's only to complain about something," he said, "but not today. Oh, no. They couldn't speak highly enough of you, and your program. They said they were putting their names on the waitlist for the next session. Oh! And they said how lucky Jackson was to have a teacher of your caliber and that we should never let you go."

"Well, I'm not going anywhere," Sarah laughed.

"And I wouldn't have it any other way," Mr. Coles said.

❧

So it was that on this late summer afternoon, as the parched furnace of the New Mexico sun baked the streets of Phoenix, Sarah stood in the sidelines in the crisp climate- controlled conference room standing ready to walk out on stage in front of a large screen to deliver her keynote presentation. The audience was just settling back after the break and one of the conference organizers was making a few housekeeping announcements about the rest of the schedule for the afternoon and the social networking event for the early evening.

"Are you nervous?" an assistant asked her.

"I thought I would be nervous," Sarah said, "but I'm actually excited. I can't wait to get out there."

"You program is so interesting," the young woman said, "I was reading about it when I was copying your supporting notes for the audience."

"Thank you," Sarah said, "that means a lot. I put some effort into that paper."

"I think it will be a hit," the assistant said, "I'm Debbie. I was the one who sent you the letter?"

"Really?" Sarah said, "well, thank you, Debbie. It was you I spoke with on the phone then?"

"Yes," the assistant laughed, "and I remember you seemed very surprised to be invited. You thought I had the wrong person."

"I did," Sarah said, "it was a surprise."

"It was pretty funny," she said, "I even double-checked with my boss to make sure I hadn't sent it to the wrong person!"

GALE A. LEE & ALICE M. SPENCE

"Really?" Sarah said, "no wonder you remember me. I guess it checked out then. It was the right person."

"Oh yes," she said, "we had the letter from your colleague and then followed up with the recommendation from your principal."

"A letter from my colleague?" Sarah was intrigued.

"Yes, that's how we first heard about your program; a teacher from your school recommended it for our conference. She thought my boss should know about it."

"You don't happen to remember the name, do you"?

"Not right now, but I can look it up," she said, "wait, I remember the first name was Amberlee. It's one of those names you remember. Pretty name. Do you know her?"

"Yes, I do," Sarah said.

Amberlee. Somehow, in a roundabout sort of way it made sense. All this time that Amberlee had resisted Sarah's direct attempts to enlist her to *Quality Conversations*, Sarah had been preaching to the converted. Amberlee not only had believed in the program, she had felt so strongly about it that she had recommended it to the conference and never mentioned a word about it. Even when her personal difficulties had prevented her from embracing the full benefit of *Quality Conversations* for herself, she had seen the value of it enough to highlight it to others.

Sarah did not feel any of this as a personal triumph, but as validation that *Quality Conversations* was a cause worth pursuing in its own right. It touched people in different ways, even those who resisted it at first. Maybe that was it. The people who fought the hardest were the ones who needed it most. She felt her smile spreading over her

177

from the inside, her eyes stinging with emotion. At this precise moment the audience went quiet as Sarah heard her name being introduced over the sound system. Her smile sparkled bright on her face as the spotlight followed her confident steps to the podium. Sarah was exactly where she was meant to be.

Part 3: The Four Pillars of a Quality Conversation

The Model

A Quality Conversation

"A quality conversation is one with two or more persons desiring to consciously and intentionally engage, learn, and understand each other's issue or concern; thereby ensuring that all individuals receive a successful end result."

—Gale A. Lee and Alice M. Spence

The underlying factors that conspire to deteriorate valuable communication can rear up anywhere like weeds in a neglected garden. Good communication does not just simply materialize, as if by magic; it is the result of dedicated and sustained work. Some people have a natural inclination to acquire these skills; others need to learn them and persevere until they master them.

The good news is that once learned these skills are invaluable tools not only at work but on every level of our interaction with others at home, on the playground, in our family time, and in our closest relationships. We can learn through having quality conversations that communication and relationship development are closely connected.

181

A good starting point to improve our communication is to shine a light on the impact that our conversations have on others. From that place of awareness, we can move forward to train our thinking by using the four pillars of *Quality Conversations* so that we build the best possible foundation for our communication. Once this foundation is solid, we can coach others by intentionally utilizing the four pillars of QC and spreading the message around.

How important is it to learn these pillars? If you just think about it for a moment, not a day goes by without you having a conversation at work, at home, on the phone, via the Internet, and even with yourself. There is a goal, a message, what it is that you wish to communicate, whether it is a problem, a solution, a concern, or just to relate an event and share data.

Every time you communicate, you navigate through a series of options. How do I say this? What do I withhold and what do I disclose? Hundreds of decisions go into each exchange. Without a map, a pattern, a blueprint for a conversation, it is almost inevitable to lose your way and stumble. The four pillars of quality conversation provide this blueprint so that you can easily find your way even through the most difficult conversations. It helps you define the critical questions and find the answers. The model shapes where you are at present with a particular concern, helps you analyze the options and alternatives available, and it helps you guide and realize your commitment to quality conversations.

182

The Benefits of a Quality Conversation

The teachers hired today are the teachers that will help shape the next generation. They will have a critical impact on the success of the people that will be in charge of running things in the future and therefore the importance of their role in society cannot be underestimated. Any support that teachers can be afforded in the unfolding of their mission is an investment in the health of our communities. Their success can be cemented by providing them with a comprehensive and coherent professional development program. Since the ultimate purpose of any educational institution is the success and achievement of its students, any effort that is made to improve student achievement, even the smallest initiative, is a step in the right direction. The main factor for any progress in student achievement boils down to the teachers, their qualifications, what the teacher knows, and what the teacher is able to communicate in the classroom (Greenwald, Hedges, & Laine, 1996). Studies that use value-added student achievement data have found that student achievement gains are much more influenced by a student's assigned teacher than other factors like class size and class composition (Darling-Hammond & Youngs, 2002). Effective teachers manage to produce better achievement regardless of which curriculum materials, pedagogical approach, or reading program is selected (Allington, 2003).

Quality conversations that begin in the classroom have an extended effect on all aspects of our lives. The benefits of a *Quality Conversation* can:

- Produce life and build up people
- Engage people to become creative and positive
- Motivate and empower others
- Increase self-esteem and confidence
- Develop leaders and great employees

The Four Pillars of Quality Conversations: The Model

- Active Listening
- Asking Powerful Questions
- Giving and Receiving Constructive Feedback
- Reflection

The Challenges of Managing Conversations: Case Studies

Now you have the framework. Let's look at each pillar in action.

Pillar 1: Active Listening

Active Listening is the foundation for a quality conversation. It sets the stage for the other pillars to be applied successfully. The physical attributes of active listening are eye contact, open posture, and facial expressions. The listener should be considering the speaker's thoughts and feelings during the conversations.

Case 1:

John is forty-five. He is a computer engineer with an outstanding work ethic. So far his job has involved working on projects, and thanks to his remarkable performance, he has recently been promoted to the position of department manager. Two months into his new role, John was caught by surprise. Seemingly out of the blue two of his most valued veteran staff members put in a request to be transferred to another department. Why might they want to leave?

Case Analysis:

When John took over as head of the department he continued to treat his job as a project, not realizing that he was no longer in charge of putting together the parts of a system but that he was now in charge of people. As a new-

186

comer he approached the department as a system, so he looked at anything that needed fixing and decided what needed to be done and then instructed the staff accordingly. The exercise of listening did not take priority. It is little wonder that the two staff members that had the most experience, the people that felt they had the most to contribute to the department, felt alienated in what they perceived as not being heard. When John asked them what they wanted, they hadn't mentioned that they were unhappy before putting in the formal transfer. They both said that they didn't think he would be interested in listening to their reasons. As soon as John was made aware of this fact, the whole dynamic changed. He asked them to put their transfer request on hold for two weeks with the commitment that if they still felt the same way by then, he would gladly sign off on and support the transfer. They both agreed. It didn't take two weeks for the two of them to withdraw their request completely.

Once John put listening at the top of his priorities, the quality of the conversation opened a whole new level of communication. He created daily "flash-meetings" where for ten minutes every morning over a cup of coffee he listened to what the staff had to say. Listening created the opportunity for John to learn what was important and for his staff to learn what the goals and objectives were. This simple procedure lowered the level of anxiety of people who needed to be heard. The two staff members went back to a feeling of value and acceptance. Listening is a powerful tool because it allows people to deal with the content of the message instead of getting hung up on their relationship with the messenger. John continues to sit and listen intuitively; this allows him to reflect, develop powerful questions, and offer feedback so that he can clearly identify possible solutions. He has become twice as effective as a manager as he was before as a project engineer.

Pillar 2: Asking Powerful Questions

"Asking powerful questions creates more insightful and empowered results (Scott Andrews)."

Case 2:

Aaron is an eighteen-year-old graduating senior who lives with both his parents. In August he will be preparing to move to the next level of schooling – college. As the date approaches his parents realize that there are many challenges to new college students so they want to have a conversation with their son about any concerns he has related to college, but every attempt at conversation ends up with an "I know," or a "thanks, I hear you" from their son. They fear that he is merely going through the motions of listening to them, but that there is no real communication going on. How might they improve this conversation?

Case Analysis:

Parents of small children are used to finding the "right" answer as their children keep discovering the mysteries of the world and bombarding them with questions. As their children grow up and become more independent, however, some parents have trouble adjusting to the change. It is now as important to ask questions, as it is to answer them. If asking good questions is so critical, why don't most parents spend more time and energy on discovering what the right questions are and then framing them?

Even in the classroom, students are presented with question after question where they need to find the right answer, but they are not so often exposed to the skill of formulating a question to obtain the information they need. It is no wonder that question skills are not highly developed in our conversations. So far Aaron's parents had approached their conversation as a one-way flow of information. They spoke, Aaron listened, and there the conversation ended. One day at a garage sale Aaron's mother spotted a small hand-decorated plate that read, "Whoever asks questions will never get lost. – Ancient Senegalese Proverb." It made her think of their conversations with Aaron, and it occurred to her that they had failed to ask him the right questions. She bought the little plate on the spot and hung it in the kitchen. That weekend as they all sat around the table for a relaxed pancake breakfast, Aaron's parents asked their son if he had any areas of concern about college life and leaving home. She just asked the question and then remained silent, providing enough space for Aaron to formulate his ideas. First came a shrug from Aaron as he lowered his gaze down to his pancakes. A few minutes later, however, Aaron asked them if they thought he would do well in college.

Instead of replying right away, Aaron's mother kept the conversation open by asking him to define his question further. "Do well in what respect?" The way the conversation was naturally evolving, Aaron followed through and

189

opened up to his parents as they learned about his insecurities. He had a great academic record so he was not worried about that. He was more interested in the social aspects of this change in his life, how he would make new friends, if he would lose touch with his old friends, what to expect from life away from home. Aaron's parents were also reassured to know that he had been listening to every word they had spoken about the challenges and pitfalls that may lie ahead. He had a good head on his shoulders as he was already planning his budget, his class schedule, and even frequent trips home. By the end of that breakfast, they were all feeling much more confident about the future and about their ability to rely on each other in a quality conversation.

Direct questions go straight to the point.

Examples:

What will you do if…
    How will your decision impact your college experience?

Open questions let the person direct the conversation.

Examples:

Tell me more about …
    So what do you think college life will be like?

GALE A. LEE & ALICE M. SPENCE

Ownership questions focus on taking ownership and being proactive.

Examples:

When you encounter problems, what can you do about them?

Some experiences build character. What experiences might you encounter that can build your character?

Revealing questions help the person look at the issue in a new way.

Examples:

What do you want your grade point average to look like at the end of this school year?

If you were in need, who would you call if you could not get in touch with us?

Pillar 3: Giving and Receiving Constructive Feedback
Case 3:

Adam is confronted with a crisis the day before his presentation before the CEO. The yearly inventory numbers are not matching and his warehouse foreman has called in sick. He has just a few hours to find the source of the discrepancy, finish his report, and email it to the head office.

Case Analysis:

Feedback is an extremely important part of communication. So far Adam's management style had concentrated

191

on directing, following up, measuring, and correcting. The main flaw in his communication cycle was the fact that he did not have an organized way to collect feedback coming back to him from the warehouse floor. These people were the eyes and ears of the company; they were in contact with the everyday small things that went right or wrong. If Adam had had a system for collecting their feedback on seemingly small incidents, he would have noticed a pattern that was emerging in significant shortages from one of their suppliers. On an isolated basis—one by one—these shortages were not important, but by the end of the year, they had accumulated and posed an accounting problem.

When Adam headed down to the warehouse floor to see what was wrong, he found to his dismay that every one of the employees had noticed these small shortages, but they had never mentioned it to each other or their foreman. They seemed isolated, and there was no line of communication asking them to bring back their observations up to their foreman. Since the quantities were not big enough to report as an anomaly according to the existing procedure, the problem just kept on occurring under the radar.

Feedback is not only important when things are going wrong; it is equally critical when things are going right. Many people don't think enough about providing feedback when there is something good to report, finding it more natural to flag something that is failing. Feedback helps us become aware of situations and aware of how our actions and behavior is being perceived. In order to be effective, feedback must be clear and not ambiguous. Sweeping remarks are to be avoided, such as "unprofes-

192

sional" or "terrible driver or "always late," because they are neither helpful nor specific. Measured and precise feedback is priceless. Another factor to keep in mind when giving feedback is to avoid being emotional as much as possible. Feedback given when a person is angry, upset, or tired will not result in a productive atmosphere for communication. This applies also to the receiver. Waiting for the right moment and using objective feedback will result in a direct improvement in the quality of the conversation.

Pillar 4: Reflection
Case 4:

Megan volunteered at a homeless shelter on weekends. She mainly helped sorting out donated supplies, organizing the kitchen before the meal, and on special occasions she would also help out serving. While she couldn't say that she enjoyed the work, she felt that she was giving her time for a good cause and that made her feel like she was a valuable member of the community. Increasingly, however, she was at odds with the head of the shelter, who carried herself with an abrupt attitude and never showed any emotion towards the people she was helping. She finally confronted her supervisor one day and told her she was asking to be assigned to another shelter. The lady didn't even flinch; she just told her that she could come back if she changed her mind. Megan changed shelters only to find that the new shelter was completely disorganized and things were being wasted right and left. The atmosphere was so chaotic that it even got a little turbulent when meals were delayed or supplies went missing. She had jumped from the frying pan into the fire.

193

Case Analysis: What is reflection?

Megan realized she had not appreciated the leadership skills required to maintain such a complex organization running. Now that time had passed and she was able to reflect on it, she had a renewed appreciation for her former supervisor. What she had perceived as uncaring had actually cared better for the people the supervisor was in charge of. Megan had failed to take the communication in the right context, given the severe challenges of the environment. When we are involved in a communication process that happens over time, with people that we see and interact on a regular basis, it is helpful to think of it as an extended conversation. We need to listen, ask questions, give and receive feedback—then start all over again.

One important factor to consider as well is that in order for this conversation to have any quality, we will need to absorb and process all these instances of listening, all these questions, and all these feedback. If we don't, then our understanding will not evolve to the next level. Analytical reflection can be thought of as the process of looking at a patchwork quilt. If we are always looking at the small detail level, stitch by stitch, we will never be able to recognize the pattern as a whole picture. Reflection can take time. It can be active, as in the case of analyzing a paper for a presentation or writing an essay on a subject, or passive, when the facts and thoughts naturally settle and open our eyes to a new and expanded realization. Reflection can help us shed preconceived ideas and acquire new points of view. It can help us turn external data into internal knowledge.

Epilogue: The Campaign for Quality Conversations

We are firm believers that if more people engaged in quality conversations on a regular basis the workplace would be a better place. Being educators this is where our focus started, but it doesn't need to end there. In fact, we are committed to making the world a better place, one conversation at a time. Becoming a teacher involves a certain amount of selflessness, a giving of oneself for the improvement of others. Through this book we aim to extend that reach, to give of ourselves to others with the idea that one day you, the reader, will find yourself applying one or all of the pillars mentioned in this book and having a breakthrough in the quality of your conversations. By helping people communicate, we hope that we can help them move forward in their chosen path, whichever their chosen profession. We also aim to recruit them as messengers of the model, to pollinate and multiply endless conversations, and share the model with those people who cross their paths. This book is just the beginning!

195

About the Authors

Gale A. Lee, Ph.D., is an educator who has spoken at national and international conferences. Her dissertation focused on new teacher induction programs in Hampton Public Schools. Her research has focused on teacher retention, family engagement, and quality conversations. Dr. Lee has twenty-two years of experience in public education as a teacher, college professor, and central administrator. She is presently the Senior Director of Compensatory Education Programs for Norfolk Public Schools in Norfolk, VA.

Dr. Lee has served on the Tidewater Community College Board as a member and chair. She is a certified leadership coach and member of many educational and civic organizations. Most recently she was awarded the National Sorority of Phi Delta Kappa, Inc. Eastern Region Citation Award for her active engagement in educational pursuits serving young people. She also trains and works with pre-service teachers using "REAL Talk", a training program that focuses on quality conversations. Prior to serving in the educational field, she worked as a corrective therapist at the Veteran Administration Hospital in Marion, IN. She resides in Hampton, VA.

197

Alice M. Spence, M.S.W. is a professional life coach, and the founder of Uncovering Visions and Aspirations, LLC, Life Coaching & Consulting Services. She specializes in working with youth and adults who are committed to realizing and discovering their academic and personal goals and dreams. She is a licensed school counseling director, licensed substance abuse counselor, educational consultant, and a dynamic conference speaker. Alice has over twenty-nine years of extensive experience in individual and group counseling, consulting, leadership, academic and college planning, and people and program development.

She presently serves as a school counseling and guidance director at Lafayette-Winona middle school in the Norfolk Public Schools' system in Norfolk, VA. She has also served as new teacher mentor/coach at her previous middle school. During Alice's previous career, she was a commissioned officer in the U S Army active duty for eleven years, where she served as an executive company commander and platoon leader to hundreds of soldiers and junior officers. She presently acts as a ministry advisor at her church to other ministries including Christian education, teens, and women's ministries. Alice was recently selected as one of Norfolk Public Schools' 2011 Outstanding Employee of the Week and was awarded the Hampton University 2009 Exemplary Educator Award in school counseling. In addition, Alice was selected as a semi-finalist for the 2008 American School Counselor Association Counselor of the Year. She has written many articles regarding education, youth topics, and quality conversations. Alice resides with her daughter, Joselyn, and pit bull, Nyia, in Suffolk, VA.

198

Bibliography

Eric E. Vogt, Juanita Brown, and David Isaaca, "The Art of Powerful Questions: Catalyzing Insight, Innovation, and Action", *The Whole System Associates*, December 2003.

Lisa Lambert. "Half of Teachers Quit after 5 years," *Washington Post*, May 9 2006.

Sara Lawrence-Lightfoot. The Essential Conversation. Random House 2003.

Richard Allington, "What I've Learned About Effective Reading Instruction From a Decade of Studying Exemplary Elementary Classroom Teachers." Phi Delta Kappan. June (2002).

L. Darling-Hammond and P. Youngs, Defining "Highly Qualified Teachers:" What does "scientifically based research" tell us? *Educational Researcher*, 31 (2002): 13-25.

R. Greenwald, L.V. Hedges, and R.D. Laine. "The Effect of School Resources on Student Achievement" *Review of Educational Research* 66 (1996): 361-396.

"The Art of Focused Conversation," by Brian Stanfield, web: http://ica-associates.ca/.

Ronald Carter and Michael McCarthy, The Lost Art of Conversations.

Alice M. Spence, "Helping My Son", Tidewater Parent Magazine, November (2009), 55.

Gale A. Lee, Ph.D. "Conversations", RedLine Beauty Newsletter, Fall (2007), 1.

Chaim Feuerman, "Listening as Leadership", Principal Leadership, March (2008), 64-65.

Elizabeth Bolton: Leadership Development: Giving and Receiving feedback, University of Florida, December 2008. Web Site at http://edis.ifas.ufl.edu.

Fuller, Deena S. What is reflection? Tennessee State University, Nashville, TN, June (2010). *www.tnstate.edu.*

Harry K. Wong, Induction Programs that keep new teachers teaching and improving: 2004.

Michael A. Harris., PhD. Family Therapy: Home VS Office. June 2006.

Dr. Joseph Umidi, Transformational Coaching (Maitland, Florida: Xulon Press)2005.

Dr. Joseph Umidi, Confirming the Pastoral Call: A Guide to matching candidates and congregations, (Grand Rapids: Michigan Kregel Publications) 2000.

Dr. B. Courtney McBath, Maximizing your Marriage (Lake Mary, Florida, Creation House Press) 2002.